THE LIES OF OUR TIME

ANTHONY ESOLEN

THE LIES

OF OUR TIME

SOPHIA INSTITUTE PRESS
Manchester, New Hampshire

Cover by Updatefordesign Studio

Cover image: *Bare Tree Lot* by Sergey Nikolaev (@kefiijrw) (UnSplash)

Sophia Institute Press
Box 5284, Manchester, NH 03108
1-800-888-9344
www.SophiaInstitute.com

Sophia Institute Press is a registered trademark of Sophia Institute.

paperback ISBN 978-1-64413-802-1

ebook ISBN 978-1-64413-803-8

Library of Congress Control Number: 2023945542

First printing

Contents

THE LIES OF OUR TIME

Introduction

On Good Friday, one of the traditional ten petitions in my church is a prayer for those who do not believe in God, that they may find Him "by sincerely following all that is right." That implies that there is a right way to go, a truth to seek. "I am a friend to Plato," said Aristotle of his beloved friend and teacher, "but a better friend to the truth." "O Truth, Truth," cried Augustine, "how did the marrow of my soul, even at that time, pant after you, all while those men," the Manichaeans he had fallen in with, "were sounding your name to me, so often and in so many ways, with the voice alone, and in a load of heavy books!" As the body hungers for good food, so does the mind hunger for truth.

I have an abiding love for mathematics, from when I was a small boy. Part of its appeal to me is that it opens out a realm where beauty and truth appear to be in wonderful harmony. Legend has it that when Pythagoras saw, with a flash of insight as he looked at a square nested within four right triangles, the theorem that bears his name, he was so profoundly moved by it that he considered it a holy thing, one to speak of only to his devoted followers, in awe. We should remember here that the Greeks did not have a system of numerals. For them, a number was a length, and its square was a square, and its cube was a cube. Their mathematicians thought in terms of geometric objects. They manipulated circles and squares, triangles and other polygons, prisms and spheres, and other solids. Pythagoras saw his theorem as a matter of beautiful and surprising relations, bringing order where no order had been expected.

Another legend has it that when the mathematician and inventor Archimedes was taking a bath, he suddenly grasped the law governing an object's displacement of water, and he leaped from the bath, crying out, "Eureka"—meaning, "I've found it!" Mathematicians themselves judge proofs by their beauty, and they sense that the beauty implies a further reach than they are aware of, and further realms of discovery. And they do speak of discovery, not of invention. Whatever their stated philosophy may be, when they work they are realists, and they treat the things they investigate as real, though impossible to see with the eye, or touch with the hand, or measure on a scale. They find the truth invigorating.

I find it invigorating, too, most especially when it soars beyond the material world. Indulge me a minute or two, my reader. I have asked myself the oddball question, "Is the set of numbers that man can specify individually by any finite means countably infinite, or uncountably infinite?" That is, can you match each element in the set, one by one, with the natural numbers 1, 2, 3, and so on, and get to all the numbers that way? That is what is called the countably infinite. Or is it impossible to do that—as it is impossible with all the numbers, rational and irrational, between 1 and 1.00001? That is what is called the uncountably infinite. I believe it is the former, that you *can* do that matching, at least theoretically, and if that is true, there is, as I see it, a tremendous consequence. We are used to hearing people say, glibly, that unless you can demonstrate something, either by logical deduction, as in mathematics, or by empirical investigation, as in the sciences, you cannot know that it exists. But if the conjecture is correct, there will be numbers, and indeed almost every number will be of this sort, that you will never be able to specify by any means. They will exist, but you won't even be able to name which ones they are. It is, apparently, an open conjecture. Still, I wish to know the truth of it. These things please me, as sweet things please the palate.

And far be it from me to look down on what we *can* know by observation. Today, I saw a rare pileated woodpecker climbing up one of our pine trees, eating grubs, I suppose, from large holes it pounded out with its bill. I wanted to know whether it was male or female. It was the latter. I wanted to find the mate somewhere nearby, since I have usually seen them in pairs. At other times, I walk into the woods in summer, just when the wild raspberries are ripening, and I hear the high, thin, mouselike call of the otherwise mute cedar waxwings. Most of their diet consists of berries. And I watch them; I watch the male court the female by finding her a berry and feeding it to her, and that, too, delights me, because it is another window into reality, and it is another sweet thing. This courtship of the female by the male is, I know very well, denied by people in our time, who seem to believe that a man can appeal to a woman without showing the slightest capacity to provide for her and her children — as if the demands of biological nature could be waved aside with a stroke of an ideological wand. Or I listen to someone who knows the difference between hemlock and maple, and what each wood is good for, and he shows me why, and that is like good bread, plain and sturdy and nourishing. I can imagine such birds and trees as have never existed, and that may be a different kind of good thing, but it cannot, of itself, satisfy my hunger. I want to know the truth.

The English word *truth*, as it turns out, is a cousin to our word *tree*, and both are cousins of the Latin adjective *durus*, meaning "hard," "solid." The truth is like an oak rooted firmly and deeply in the earth. You can depend on it. It is not going to give way at a little pressure. Carpenters call a wall they are raising *true* if it stands plumb, at right angles to the base. And *right*, a cousin of Latin *rectus*, suggests what is straight, upright, not crooked, not hanging aslant. If you are going to buy a plot of land from someone, you want him to be *straight* with you, not a *crook*, not like a beam of wood that is twisted and that will begin to bow under great weight. If he is a crook, a thoroughgoing liar and cheat, he will be what the Romans called *pravus*, "crooked," the adjective from which we ultimately derive our English words *depraved* and *depravity*. If you have a *queer* feeling in your gut, you cannot rest easy; and it is no surprise that the word is related to Latin *torquere*, to "twist"; we say that our stomach is in knots, or, of someone who enjoys what is wicked, that he has a *twisted* mind.

I know plenty of people who will boast of their grave sins, so long as the wickedness has some flair to it or involves the appearance or the exercise of power. I do not know anyone who boasts of being a liar. To boast that you are a liar seems like boasting that your very existence is a negative; like boasting that you are an un-being. It is most instructive that when Jesus names what distinguishes Satan from other beings, it is that "he was a murderer from the beginning," "a liar and the father of lies" (John 8:44). But although we say that we want the truth, what we typically do is to raise a fence around the portion of the truth we will admit or concede or proclaim, while keeping the rest out. That persistent trouble is exacerbated in our time. For many of the fences we raise are not personal but ideological and political, designed not just to silence a nagging voice within that tells you that you have done wrong, but to rule out of bounds whole realms of truth that people do not wish to acknowledge. A man may kill his enemy because he hates him, or because he wants his property or his wife. These are evil motives, and yet they are humanly understandable. But the Nazis could kill, with programmatic coldness, millions of Jews and others, only because they had accepted the great lie that ruled out of existence the humanity of their victims; and this is what the Soviets did to their political prisoners, what the Maoists did to people who held on to ancient traditions, and what Americans do to their own children whom they do not want. These are lies that sap the humanity of the liars themselves. The details of their arguments, such as they are, are wearisome, and they hardly matter, because once ideology — the evil parody of and substitute for religion — sets roots in your soul, you can find reasons to justify anything and backfit your argument to lead where you want to go. Indeed, in the United States, we Americans assume that that is what our Supreme Court does all the time. You choose the destination, and then you pretend that it is where your reasons have led you, when the truth is that your reason has been suborned and gives in false evidence, in the service of some desire. "Reason," says the poet John Donne, describing his soul as a walled town taken prisoner by the enemy, and praying to God to deliver it by force, "your viceroy in me, me should defend, / But is captived, and proves weak, or untrue" ("Holy Sonnet 14," 7–8). Thus does the Court embody on a grand stage the drama of the individual man in the grip of the liar. For just this cause, the dyspeptic John Adams considered Tom Paine's lauded "Reason" to be a whore: the atheistic philosopher, he believed, had pretended to raise reason to the status of a god, when all that such reason did was to provide arguments for the appetite.

But the range of reason extends over almost the whole of human experience. Employed aright, it is dispositive, it is an element of man's conscience, telling us what we *must not* do, though we very much want to do it, and what we *must* do, though we very much want *not* to do it. Again, it is not to be bound to what I can demonstrate by mathematical definition and reasoning, or to what I can show by empirical tests. It extends to how we should live our lives; to what justice is, and mercy; to what duties we owe to our kin, our neighbors, our countrymen, and the stranger who shows up at our door; to how we should use the goods the world provides, including our fellow creatures the animals and plants; to what men and women are to be in relation to one another; to the special consideration we owe to children, to the weak, the vulnerable, the foolish, and the sickly; to what we should rejoice in and what should bring us sorrow; to all affairs of business and education and art; to the duties we owe to our Creator. I say so not merely as a Christian but as a human being, and all the great pagan thinkers will agree with me here, from Greece and Rome to India, China, and Japan. People who say otherwise are the outliers.

And yet, in our time, falsehood has many an advantage over truth. For the search for truth requires patience, probity, a calm mind, and the humility to accept it when you find it and to change your ways accordingly. The person in love with truth will hold himself to *higher* standards of honor than those around him do. When I was an undergraduate at Princeton, we had an honor code that was genuinely liberating. The professor need not stay in the room to glower over us as we took our exams. We were our own proctors. You could leave the room at any time, even taking the exam with you. But I have recently read an article in the student newspaper that attacks that honor code as fostering an environment of hostility and as being especially harmful to minority students. Not once in the article does the author acknowledge the evils of lying and cheating. She is not in love with truth, and so she reaches for excuses and turns what ought to be a mark of high honor into a weapon of oppression. It is impossible to imagine Booker T. Washington, a man of scrupulous honor, encouraging such a slipshod attitude in his students. But the irritant of political envy and resentment is all too ready to turn what is dishonorable into a downright virtue.

Everything that makes us less patient, that makes us touchier and quicker to seek and to take offense, proud and defiant in our ways; everything, too, that makes us assert our individuality against the common wisdom of mankind, especially as that wisdom is handed on to us in the form of sacred tradition; everything that keeps us in a permanent and none too promising adolescence makes us both more vulnerable to falsehood and more eager to spread it, with bullhorns sometimes, and sometimes with sheer governmental power. I am writing here, then, not simply to affirm several fundamental truths that many people wish to deny, to ignore, or to efface from human consciousness, but to remind myself and everyone else of the ways of truth and how truth must be sought.

THE FIRST LIE

There Is No God

So DOES THE psalmist say: "The fool says in his heart, 'There is no God'" (14:1).

It is the fundamental lie of our time. That is the case, even though declared atheists are rather few. What does it mean?

Let us suppose that the person who says so means that God does not exist. We must then inquire what he means by that proper name, God. We may dismiss his equivocations. We will not permit him to say that he does not believe in God, just as a Christian does not believe in Mister Zeus. That is because *no Christian believes in God just as an ancient Greek might have believed in Zeus.* They are entities of wholly separate orders. I stress this point, which atheists themselves used to acknowledge in the days when people might have read books, because we now often hear from ill-read and ill-tempered people that to believe in God is like believing in jinn and fairies or a sky god, or something else that people can laugh at. Indeed, the now common label "sky daddy" is a dishonest attempt to evade the issue by means of little thought and much ridicule.

"Why are you laughing at that picture?" says Lucy to Charlie Brown and Linus, who are sitting on the floor by an open book.

"Because we don't understand it," they reply.

Zeus was never understood as other than a large and powerful being, not as the absolute. Zeus was born, and therefore he was not eternal. Zeus could be tricked for a time, as when his wife Hera distracted him with her beauty so that he lay with her in a golden cloud while the Greeks were winning the day in their battle with the Trojans. Therefore, he was not omniscient. Indeed, he was sometimes ruled by the desire he shared with mortal men, horses, dogs, and cats, so he was not all-good, much less all-admirable. Hence he took on the shape of a bull to ravish the girl Europa, and he sent down his eagle to Mount Ida to sweep up to his throne the beautiful Trojan boy Ganymede. Zeus was subject to the Fates, as when he wept at the death of his son Sarpedon in the Trojan War, and could do nothing to assist him, and therefore he was not omnipotent. He was, we might say, a creature. I do not *simply* mean that he was a creature of man's imagination. I mean that as that imaginary being, Zeus was thought to inhabit the same plane of being as do other creatures. He is the greatest being in the world, perhaps, but he's still *in* the world, finite, set off against other such finite beings. If you scaled the peak of Mount Olympus, you might run into him. So you didn't.

The poet Hesiod, in his *Theogony*—that is, "the birth of the gods"—portrays Zeus's rise to power as a combination of skill in warfare and shrewd political alliances. The young god's significance is bound to the peculiar and dynamic way of life the Greeks were in the process of inventing, that of the self-governing polis, as partly in conflict with an older way of life, one more firmly bound up with blood loyalties. Their most profound meditations upon the old stories of the gods are meant to open to men's eyes the possibility, and the precariousness, of a smallish society united by a common sense of kinship, and governed by reason, discourse, self-mastery, and, of course, military power. I might go so far as to say that I do indeed "believe in Zeus," taking the figure, as he is portrayed in the great plays of Aeschylus and Sophocles, as representing the great but provisional triumph of that Greek way of life. When the polis died, so did Zeus.

In the same way, the *Enuma Elish* of ancient Babylon tells of how Marduk, the tutelary god of the city, rose to power by uniting a few reasonably decent deities under his military leadership, vanquishing the wicked sea goddess Tiamat and her consort Kingu, and fashioning the world from her scattered members and mankind from her consort's blood. Marduk too, then, is bound to a place, an empire, and a way of life. To "believe in" Marduk is about the same as being a Babylonian citizen or slave in the days of Babylon's might. I do not mean that you would be *likely* to believe or *commanded* to believe in him. I mean that Marduk makes no sense outside of Babylon, nor would the Babylonians themselves understand you if you asked them whether someone three thousand miles away should believe in him. It would be like asking them whether someone three thousand miles away should send money to buy silken robes for Babylon's priests. What would be the point?

And what about the gods that are bound to some natural phenomenon? Take the corn god of the Hurons, Hiawatha. Why is it that no one can now "believe" in Hiawatha? One answer is that the revelation of God has returned nature to its proper and creaturely place in the universe. But another answer is that where corn does not grow, Hiawatha makes no sense. Would the Inuit seal hunters sing to a god of a plant that cannot grow where they live? Would the suggestion even make sense to them? Or how can one see a Hiawatha in thousands of acres in Illinois, given to the soybean and ultimately to the thousands of products manufactured from its fibers and oil? The ancient Egyptians saw life springing up every year from the fertile mud of the flooded Nile. They were wrong to identify the Nile with a divinity—with Osiris, and with the Pharaoh or "Great House" on earth who will become Osiris when he dies and who guarantees good floodwaters. They were perhaps not so far wrong when they saw *divinity at work* in the Nile, for the river is sublime, and all the creatures of nature, mountains and hills, snow and rain, rivers and the sea, praise the Lord. If, then, you ask whether I believe in Osiris flowing gently to the sea, my answer is no, I do not, but if you ask whether I share, in some small way, the ancient Egyptian sense that divinity is at work there, and whether the fit response to that work is an appreciative awe and gratitude, the answer is yes, though our current way of life makes it extraordinarily difficult for modern man to be alive to such wonder.

The False Alternatives

Now there are two most striking things about God, as we are introduced to Him in Genesis. The first is that He is bound to no theogony and no mythologized establishment of a city or empire. He has no ancestors. He has no beginning. Rather He *is the beginning*: "In the beginning God created the heavens and the earth" (Gen. 1:1). The Hebrew does not suggest that God was merely first in a series of beings or events. The root of the Hebrew *reshith*—"beginning"—is *rosh*, meaning "head" or "chief," well translated by the Jewish scholars of the Greek Septuagint as *arche*: a beginning as a *foundation* or *governing principle*. When God creates the light, and the Hebrew verb *bara* is, in Scripture, predicated of God alone, He needs nothing to create it out of. Rather, so to speak, He pours being into what had no being. He says, punning on His own name, *Yehi 'or*, and there was light. And of that morning and evening were, says the sacred author, *yom echad*, not just the first day but "one day," with the strong stress on the final word, *one*. We may hear an echo of the holiest of Jewish prayers: "Hear, O Israel, the Lord, the Lord thy God is *one*." There is in God no before or after or besides.

The second thing to notice is that God is bound to no feature of the natural world. He is not a sun god, because He made the sun. He is not a corn god, because He made the earth and every living thing in it. Everywhere you go in the world, wherever you investigate the pagan myths of mankind, you will find a theogony, entangled with cities and the vines that give the people their food, smudged with soil and soaked in blood. But God is, and that is all. There is none before Him, not because that happened to be so, but because it is inconceivable that it should be so. There is no *conceivable* name beyond the name that is none, the name that identifies God as being beyond identifying: "I AM WHO I AM," says God, when Moses asks for His name (Exod. 3:14). Something of the sheer power of this transcendence can be gathered from the pseudo-Areopagite, who says that God is even *beyond being*; for that keen-minded mystic feared that we might reduce Him to *a being*, one among many, and therefore circumscribed, and therefore not God.

Nor is God a civic deity. It is true that the Chosen People are established in the Promised Land, and they do build a city, Jerusalem, and God does give them laws to order their lives. People must live in communities, after all. We cannot all wander forever from feeding ground to feeding ground. But the relationship between God and the kings of Israel and Judah is fraught with conflict, because men are sinners, and because their inclination is always to fall back into the god-fertile nature religions of their neighbors, or to rely upon the city as a kind of talisman, as if God were to be bound up with stones and civic laws and a custom of ritual worship. In other words, when the sons of Israel sin, they fall back into a theogony, worshiping a cycle of birth and death as if it were absolute, or they turn to a city worship, taking God as if He were a Marduk, and Jerusalem as if it were Babylon. And we should recall, too, as Augustine reminds us in *The City of God*, that the first builder of a city that Scripture mentions is Cain, the first fratricide. Augustine was not going to miss the implications of that for Rome. We have many an ancient representation of the twin babies Romulus and Remus, sucking at the swollen teats of the she-wolf; and the legend had it also that Romulus would kill his brother Remus and be the sole ruler of the city he was founding.

Besides, just as Jeremiah foretold the destruction of Jerusalem, so did Isaiah foretell the triumph of God *beyond* Jerusalem, and not because the Jews would triumph everywhere but because the knowledge of the Lord would fill the earth, and the isles shall wait for His law, and all they from Sheba shall come, bearing gold and frankincense. Essentially, these prophecies are the same. For God is the Lord of all mankind, and the earthly Jerusalem is but a local shadow of the universal reality.

And in this sense, in our time, the atheist—who wants to suggest that the Christian or Jewish believer in God is just like the Greek who believed in Zeus or the Babylonian who believed in Marduk or the Egyptian who believed in Osiris and the semidivine Pharaoh—is himself unwittingly like the idolators that Ezekiel saw wailing over the death of the regenerate Canaanite god Tammuz, or like the Egyptians crying out, "Great House, Great House," as the Pharaoh raced in early spring along the banks of the Nile to ensure a flood of good feeding. For just as the worship of God must ultimately be conformed to His one and only necessary Being, so, too, the denial of God *must conform us to the two great things we see around us*, that is, to the creatures of the natural world or to the artifices of man the city dweller. The atheist is quite gullible; against all the evidence of history, he believes, with an almost admirable naïveté and doggedness, that political structures will redeem us, or he (usually she) attempts to gin up some submission to green things and blood, and this at a time when not one person in a thousand will ever cut the throat of an animal he has hunted or raised to put food on the table. They turn from God to Marduk or to Tammuz, from God to the mire of politics or to the mire of matter, and do not know that they have done so.

No, there is in the end only one choice. We are talking about the existence of God, such as the great traditions of human philosophy have attempted to understand Him in their striving toward the divine, and as He has been revealed in the Jewish and Christian Scriptures: the absolute Being, omnipotent, omniscient, beyond time in His eternity, existing necessarily and not by contingency, the fount and origin of all existent things, lacking none of the perfections we attribute by analogy and in a shadowy way to those existent things. Here we shall go beyond those human philosophies that err in supposing that *personhood* would set a limit upon the infinite God, for there is, as Dietrich von Hildebrand used to say, as great a chasm between the impersonal and the personal as there is between the inanimate and the animate, and God reveals Himself to Moses as *both* Being— "I am who I am"—*and* Person, for He is "the God of your father, the God of Abraham, the God of Isaac, and the God of Jacob" (Exod. 3:6). And that is why, says Jesus, we may trust that life does not end with the death of the body, for God is the God of the living, not of the dead.

Demonstrability

The question, then, is not whether this or that imaginary deity exists, but whether God exists—the absolute Being. Here we may bring into the arena the various demonstrations that God *must exist*, though I doubt that they have persuaded anyone to alter one moment of his life, to restrain or reject a single illicit desire, to move in love toward those who are not lovable, to set a single stone upon a stone for an altar or a temple of adoration, or to sing a single note in praise. That does not mean that I reject the demonstrations. Indeed, I think they are powerful, logically; most of them do indeed work.

Take, for example, the argument from contingent being. I look around me and see things that exist but that *need not exist*: it is perfectly reasonable to imagine a world in which they do not exist. Each of them has been brought into existence by some cause that itself need not have existed. But you cannot continue this relationship of dependence indefinitely. Nor does it get you out of the trouble if you gesture toward the universe and say that *that*, ultimately, is the reason why my cat Junior is curled up on his throne, sleeping. For the universe itself is only a big but finite bag filled with a great but finite number of contingent things. It can no more explain Junior than Junior can explain it. A contingent thing does not become more necessary by its being big. A set of contingent things does not become more necessary for having a lot of elements in it. But what about the laws governing that universe? Do they do all the explaining?

No, they don't, and they can't, because they themselves require explaining. I mean that their existence also is contingent. Why must the weak nuclear force be just what it is and not something slightly different? Why must the mass of a proton be almost but not quite equal to the mass of a neutron? In other words, why must the universe be this one and not some other? Physicists give the game away when, embarrassed by the exceedingly improbable combinations of properties of matter that were required to give rise to this world and Junior in it, they suppose that there is an infinite number of other universes with other sets of laws. The idea is that we merely happen to exist in one of the rare universes with propitious laws, and if our universe had not been one of those, we would not be here to discuss the matter. But that move just kicks the same problem one step down the road, or rather complicates it further, because now you have even more universes to explain, each one of them discrete, and each one *unnecessary.* And since each one must be discrete, *this* universe and *that* universe, they will be like singular points in a mathematical space, and even if you have an infinite number of such points, discrete, one by one, the chance that a random point selector would hit upon any one of them at all, rather than none of them, is zero. Imagine a number line and say for the sake of simplicity that all universes that would give rise to intelligent life must lie within a certain interval, say, the numbers between 1 and 2. Now you have a random number selector, like a peashooter aiming at the line, without any direction. The chance that the peashooter would strike that interval in its first shot is infinitesimal, less than any number you can name that is greater than 0. And no matter how often you shoot, if it is one shot at a time, one universe at a time, the infinitesimals cannot add up to anything more than the infinitesimal. Again, I am not talking about a very small number greater than 0, such as one-millionth of 1 percent. I am talking about a number less than a millionth of a millionth, and so forth, a million times: a number that can have no name, because as soon as you identify it as *some number*, it will be very small but not infinitesimal.

The other problem with this attempt to evade the "problem" — if we call it a problem to dwell in a universe governed by God rather than in a universe without meaning — is that it gives the lie to what these same scientists have been saying about themselves and their work. They say that they work only by observing empirical evidence and drawing reasonable conclusions from it. But by definition, one can have no empirical evidence of an object such as another universe that has no contact with this universe. For if you could observe that evidence, it must be within this universe, and hence not a part of some alternate universe. You must then abandon the supposition or abandon the pretense that you are a mere empirical observer. As I have said, the supposition does not get you anywhere, anyway.

But perhaps scientists should acquire some trace of humility and admit that their proper realm covers only a fraction of what human beings can know.

So then, let us return to the problem of the contingent and the necessary. Imagine, for the sake of simplicity, a universe with three objects in it, moving and reacting to one another according to a couple of laws that keep it awhile from falling together. Call the objects A, B, and C. Where did A come from? If you say it came from B, then we ask the same question of B. If you say it came from C, then we ask the same question of C. If you say that C came from "the universe," I accuse you of arguing in a circle, since the universe is nothing other than A, B, and C and the laws they obey. Where did that universe come from? You cannot say that it came from A, B, or C, or even from A, B, and C put together. If A, B, and C are not necessary, then the set that includes them is not necessary. It makes no more sense to say that the cat derives *necessary existence* from what is only a very large herd of "cats" than to say that the universe derives its *necessary existence* from the existence of a large number of individual things whose existence is not necessary. The only way to get from contingency to necessity is by way of some being whose existence is necessary. But then we are back to the classic understanding of God. Consider also: if it is *not impossible* that necessary being should exist, then necessary being *must exist*, because otherwise it would not be necessary, and you will have contradicted yourself.

There are other demonstrations too. The greatest mathematician of the twentieth century, Kurt Gödel, was a devout man, a Lutheran. His greatest single mathematical accomplishment, his incompleteness theorem, proved that any mathematical system with at least the complexity of arithmetic is necessarily incomplete, meaning that you will never exhaust the number of true things you can say about it, and that there will be some statements about it that are true that you will be unable to prove within the system itself. In other words, the attempt to reduce mathematics to a closed system—what in mathematics is analogous to the attempt to reduce all objects to the matter that makes them up and the laws they obey—was bound to fail, practically speaking. It was a fool's errand. Gödel then used the reasoning he had employed in his theorem to demonstrate the necessary existence of God—the Being possessing to an infinite degree and in an absolute way all possible perfections of any good that can be predicated of anything.

But if you do not like mathematics, you can do some research on the various miracles that have occurred and have been witnessed not by Christians alone but by skeptics, for even a single event inexplicable by natural laws must imply a Being not bound to those laws, just as, I might say, a composer who writes a song in a certain key is not bound to the laws he has himself made up for his own purposes but may well introduce notes that are not explicable in the system itself—miracle-notes, wonder-notes, notes that make for a far greater complexity and harmony than the fundamental laws of the piece could allow for. Peter Kreeft has said, shrewdly, that what makes the miracle is not just what cannot be explained by natural phenomena as we know them, or even as they can possibly be, whether we know them or not. The miracle requires a context. When tens of thousands of people at Fatima saw the sun dancing in the sky, they may have been witnessing some exceedingly rare atmospheric phenomenon, explainable by laws governing light and water vapor. Perhaps, and perhaps not, but it is almost beside the point, since they were only there in the first place because the children said there was going to be a miracle, as the Lady of their visions had told them. The miracle was thus a *sign*, implying a giver of the sign. Some strange reversal of cellular decay must have swept through the body of Lazarus like a wildfire, but even if we could say what it was, the real miracle of it is that the fire was sparked at the exact moment Jesus said, "Lazarus, come forth." It too was a *sign*, and it was intended as such by the giver of the sign. We may someday determine by what strange burst of radiation the photographic negative of the buried man was imprinted on the Shroud of Turin, with a thinness impossible to be applied by the human hand. I understand that some scientists have figured out a way to use what we *now* know about light to produce something like the image, but of course they already know what they want to produce and why they want to produce it, whereas a putative forger could not possibly know either one of those, since he had no experience of a photographic negative, the people to whom he would be presenting the image had no experience of it, and the very crafting of time, even had they the intention to make it, since they knew nothing of the complex means by which a three-dimensional body would imprint itself on a two-dimensional surface wrapped about it. That is a problem in topology to tax the wits of the most adept of modern mathematicians. Then we have features of the shroud that a medieval forger could not possibly be aware of, because they have to do with the practice and the implements of Roman torturers, and the burial customs of the Jews. And if you were aware of them — granting the impossibility for the sake of argument — there would be no point in fussing with them, since they had no value as signs for the people who would be viewing the shroud. He could or would no more fake that than he could or would fake a fossil of a long-extinct beast, of whose feeding habits neither he nor his contemporaries could know. The shroud could not be *his sign,* or any man's sign, any more than my imaginary fossil could be. But it could certainly be *God's sign*, bearing significant features that could only begin to be recognized as signs by people centuries afterward.

The miracle of the shroud is that it exists at all, a unique sign, when nothing like it, then or since, exists, and that as a sign it should testify to a unique man and a unique event—to the man, Jesus, who foretold the event itself, though the people He spoke to did not understand what He meant until after the event had occurred.

Are miracles then too specific for you? By their nature they do not admit of general laws. But then you should notice that as soon as you invoke "laws" to govern the behavior of matter, you have abandoned materialism, since the laws themselves are not material. And even though we discover the laws by studying the matter they govern, the laws are *prior in being and in cause* to the matter, more fundamental than the matter, and physicists themselves admit as much, though they do not draw the ready conclusion, which is that materialism—the belief that matter alone exists—is false. But as soon as you have admitted that immaterial things do exist, and that they are not just suppositions in the mind or human inventions, you have little recourse for your atheism. You cannot say that God cannot exist, because He cannot be seen by the eye or touched by the hand. You have foreclosed that exit.

The same thing goes for mathematical objects. God, says the author of the book of Wisdom, made the world in "measure and number and weight" (11:20), a verse that Augustine was fond of citing, and that inspired the artists, the architects, the theologians, and the poets of the Middle Ages, an influence that continued well into the Renaissance. That is why Dante says that God, though uncircumscribed, circumscribes all things (*Paradiso*, 14.30): we may say that God creates by setting the created world and all things within it into a mathematical form. How deeply this sense entered the popular imagination can perhaps be divined from the cathedrals that men of the Middle Ages built, with numbers everywhere, numbers nested in other numbers, so that the cathedral might be a microcosmos, a simultaneously vast and homely reflection of the whole universe and all human history. It pleases me to consider that number itself is inexhaustible. Mathematicians posit the set of real numbers, but they know that even the tiniest interval between two real numbers is inexhaustibly and inexpressibly rich, so much so that a plenitude of the numbers that lie, as I have conjectured, between 1 and 1.0001 will never and can never be specified by any means that man can invent. They are *uncountably* infinite—and that is no conjecture. There is no final frontier to mathematical knowledge, and that is exactly what we should expect for a creature made in the image of the infinite God.

But why should we limit knowledge to the general case? The particular, in its particularity, is itself a wonder and draws nearer to the miracle, to the infinitely inexplicable, the higher it scales the ladder of being. One proton, I suppose, is identical to another. One worm might as well be the same as another; there is no history among the vermin. The dog trembles on the brink of personality; we do talk about getting to know a dog, as we would not talk about getting to know a worm or an insect. Yet there is a limit to how far we can go, and that is not just because we do not possess the dog's sensorium. We cannot know a dog's hopes and plans, because he has none; we cannot follow the dog in his wonder at his own being, because he has no such. Still, this dog is not that dog; Spot is not Butch, and my dog Jasper of happy memory, he of the eighty tricks, was such as I never expect to see again. But when we encounter a human being, even an infant with his eyes wide open to the world, it is a profound mystery, and though there are general "laws," not actual laws but strong consistencies, that make human behavior predictable, there is no repeating a person; there is no predicting a particular person's thought. Send a probe to Saturn, by all means; learn all you can about that icy and gaseous giant; but an infinitely greater wonder is sitting in the room beside you, made in the image of God.

How Shall We Live?

Then why does the fool say in his heart, "There is no God"?

The psalmist is not speaking of theoretical knowledge. He is not saying that you are a fool if you deny the existence of God, though no doubt he would believe that such a denial is foolish. He is speaking rather of an existential claim upon us, upon our way of life, upon our actions and the reasons we give for them. The terse Hebrew statement is merely *'eyn Elohim*, with the negative, *'eyn*, suggesting a variety of absences. It may mean that something *is not there*: as when Enoch, having walked with God, is taken up by Him, and, literally, *he was not there*, meaning not that he had ceased to exist but that no one could see him anymore (Gen. 5:24). It may mean that you are *depriving someone of something*: as when Pharaoh arrogantly and cruelly says to the Hebrews, "*I will not* give you straw" to help them make their bricks (Exod. 5:10, emphasis added). It may mean that you are *missing something*: as when Sarah is said to be barren, because *not child-with-her* (Gen. 11:30). It may suggest impossibility or complete separation, as when God is called a God of faithfulness, *'eyn 'awel*, "without iniquity." It may deny a quality or an action, as it seems to do in the psalm's next verses, for after we hear that the fool has said in his heart, *'eyn Elohim*, God Himself "looks down from heaven upon the children of men, to see if there are any that act wisely, that seek after God," but "they have all gone astray, they are all alike corrupt; *there is none that does good, no, not one*" (Ps. 14:2–3, emphasis added), *'eyn 'oseh tob, 'eyn gam 'echad*.

And in that evaluation, "there is none that does good," lies the key. "Give thanks to the LORD, *for he is good*," says the psalmist (118:1, emphasis added), with that second clause taking up only two words in the Hebrew, *ki tob*. They are the same words we hear first in Genesis, when God makes the light by uttering it into existence, and God saw "that the light was good," *ki tob* (Gen. 1:4). The good-ness of the creature derives from the goodness of God. And God, as I have said, is not one among many, but simply one, *'echad*, as the sacred author says of the day when God made the light, not just that it was the first in a series of days, but *yom 'echad*, "one day" (Gen. 1:5). Now the first thing in Scripture that God declares "not good," *lo tob*, is that the man is alone (Gen. 2:18), and so He makes Eve from the side of Adam, that she should be bone of his bone and flesh of his flesh (2:23), as we hear in the first words that Adam speaks.

So we may see in the fool who says in his heart, "There is no God," the desire to do what is *not good*: and that desire sets him es-sentially against both God and his fellow man. It isolates. I am not saying that atheists are bad people. The tangle of human motives often makes it so that a man is better than his bad philosophy, or worse than his faith enjoins him to be. I have known atheists to whose care I would entrust the dearest things in the world, and I have known Christians before whom I would not leave a wallet on the table. But there is an essential connection here that must in-evitably work itself out in human affairs. To say "There is no God" is to imply that the world is *not good*—exactly what such atheists as Richard Dawkins do say, and what the atomist Lucretius, for all his genuine love for children and animals, said long ago—and that man is alone as regards the Creator to whom he should owe love and gratitude, and alone as regards other men. Again, a man may be blessed with a gentle temperament, he may like to do pleasant things for his friends, all while not believing in God and not having any rational ground for the good he does. But the falsehood will work like a poison through the body politic, and will produce, instead of self-denying and therefore self-transcending saints, meddlesome philanthropists making much of their good deeds, and instead of ordinary people who submit to the rules of virtue and who lay their sins before God, ordinary people who submit to the social fads of the time and who make sure they wash up along with the popular tide, and instead of bad people ridden with a bad conscience, perfect craters of wickedness, without fear, and without any terminus to their fall.

The Fool and His Folly

And now we return to the *fool*—Hebrew *nabal*. What does it mean?

It isn't, by far, the most common word for *fool* in Scripture. The most common, *kesiyl*, comes from an original root having to do with sluggishness and thickness: as we might call someone a "fathead." In other words, the fool is a dummy who usually has too much confidence, *kesel*, in himself, for "the tongue of the wise dispenses knowledge, but the mouths of fools [*kesilith*] pour out folly" (Prov. 15:2), and "the mind of him who has understanding seeks knowledge, but the mouths of fools feed on folly" (Prov. 15:14). The next most common, *'ewiyl*, denotes someone who is worse yet, someone who is stubborn, perverse, who never listens, for "the fear of the LORD is the beginning of knowledge," but "fools [*'ewiylim*] despise wisdom and instruction" (Prov. 1:7). Such fools are always to be condemned as morally obtuse. We might call them pigheaded or muleheaded. But there is still worse.

When Job is first afflicted by Satan, with the permission of God, his wife says to him, "Do you still hold fast your integrity? Curse God, and die." But Job replies, "You speak as one of the foolish women [*nebaloth*] would speak" (2:9–10). Such a fool is a churl, someone with no sense of moral and religious obligations, arrogant and disgraceful, base and despicable. The best illustration of it is Nabal himself, the husband of Abigail and a rich man of Carmel. David's men had been among Nabal's shepherds all the summer long, guarding them from enemies and not taking a thing for their trouble. But when came the time for sheep shearing, and David sent ten of his lads to Nabal to ask him for some hospitality, Nabal replied like a churl, "Who is David? Who is the son of Jesse? There are many servants nowadays who are breaking away from their masters. Shall I take my bread and my water and my meat that I have killed for my shearers, and give it to men who come from I do not know where?" (1 Sam. 25:10–11). At that, David calls his men to arms, but Abigail, Nabal's wife, comes out to plead with him. "Let not my lord regard this ill-natured fellow, Nabal [literally, this "man of Belial"]; for as his name is, so is he; Nabal is his name, and folly [*nebalah*] is with him" (25:25). She persuades David to hold his hand from vengeance against Nabal, who thinks perhaps that he has gotten his way by his arrogance, but soon after, when Nabal throws a feast fit for a king and is perfectly merry and drunk, Abigail tells him how David had withheld his forces, and "his heart died within him, and he became as a stone," falling dead ten days later (25:36–38).

Such a fool is neither too stupid to see the truth nor too pig-headed to turn to the truth; he is rather contemptuous of the truth, ungrateful. So we hear of Israel in Moses's final song before he dies: "Do you thus requite the LORD, you foolish [*nabal*] and senseless people? Is not he your father, who created you, who made you and established you?" (Deut. 32:6). And the fool's ingratitude and contempt are borne out in his deeds: "For the fool [*nabal*] speaks folly [*nabalah*], and his mind plots iniquity: to practice ungodliness, to utter error concerning the LORD" (Isa. 32:6).

The fool who says in his heart, "There is no God," is not too stupid to see the truth and not too set in his ways to admit he is wrong. He is ungrateful. There is something missing in him, and it is not brains. It is the sense of duty, or the acknowledgment of a gift. And just here we see most clearly the folly of our time, the lie that says, "There is no God." For the whole Western world is a great nothing, a dry and dusty soil, without the culture-forming rain of belief in the God of the Scriptures. It is to be a fool such as the young prodigal was, who thought he could have his father's living without the father (Luke 15:11–32). He spent down his inheritance until he had nothing left, and he was reduced to feeding the filthy swine for some unnamed citizen of a far country who meant nothing to him, and for whom he meant nothing. The prodigal son wished his father were dead, and that is why he insisted upon his portion of the inheritance, and the father, no doubt stung to the quick, gave the boy what he asked for. Heaven and Hell are each what we ask for; Heaven is true, and Hell is false, not in the sense that it does not exist but in the sense that it is a self-cheat, a self-swindle.

But you cannot have the heritage while you kill the father. I do not mean that you aim a dagger at your father's heart. You aim that dagger at your own. Let us think about another word in the verse, "The fool says in his heart, 'There is no God.'" What is the *heart* [Hebrew *leb, lebab*]? We are to love the Lord with all our heart and soul and mind and strength (Deut. 6:5), and that suggests that the heart is what we in English still sense it to be, the core of our being, the center of our will and our devotion. Why would the fool say so "in his heart"? Is he devoted to the notion that there is no God? What does it mean to say something in your heart? It could imply a kind of passion, a depth, a commitment, as the Lord "said in His heart" that He would not ever again curse the ground because of man, since "the imagination of man's heart is evil from his youth," and that is that (Gen. 8:21), or as when the barren Hannah, at the temple of the Lord in Shiloh, spoke "in her heart," crying out for help from God, and she was so passionate in her prayer that her lips moved but no sound came out, and the priest Eli thought she was drunk (1 Sam. 1:13). It could imply also privacy, secrecy, as when

29

Esau, having been tricked by his brother Jacob, plots vengeance against him, and he "said to himself," that is, "in his heart" [*b'libbo*], "The days of mourning for my father are approaching; then I will kill my brother Jacob" (Gen. 27:41).

And it could imply not only secrecy but dissembling, or a foolish confidence that you would never dare put into words. So, again, Moses warns the sons of Israel against attributing their victories to themselves: "Beware lest you say in your heart, 'My power and the might of my hand have gotten me this wealth'" (Deut. 8:17). He warns them also against believing that God has rewarded them for their righteousness, as if they were to say in their heart that "it is because of my righteousness that the LORD has brought me in to possess this land" (9:4). So the silliest fool feels no duty to God, but he does make a great boast of himself. He is like the rich man in Jesus' parable, fat and self-satisfied, who says, "I will pull down my barns, and build larger ones; and there I will store all my grain and my goods. And I will say to my soul, Soul, you have ample goods laid up for many years; take your ease, eat, drink, be merry." Why, the whole Western world may be like that man, with his self-sufficiency and his blind trust in material goods. But God said to him, "Fool! This night your soul is required of you" (Luke 12:18–20). The Greek word for *fool* here is *aphron*, someone who does not trouble to think—a nitwit, we might say. And yet the man hugs himself for his shrewdness and thoughtfulness. There is no fool like a sophisticated fool, with all his wealth around him.

And let us consider again what must needs happen in the soul of the *ungrateful* fool. If you look at what the old masters did, when they painted the three Graces, you will see what the poet Spenser says about it, that the Graces do not all face the same way, but two are facing toward us and one is facing from us, or the other way around, to show "that good should from us go, then come in greater store" (*The Faerie Queene*, 6.10.24.9). But what can man give to God? The same, at least, that the inferior gives to his superior, or that the receiver of a gift gives to the giver: gratitude. Gratitude is by its nature free, as free as grace itself. It participates in the grace of the gift. It makes man most like God. If, then, you are ungrateful, you do not harm the giver; you harm yourself. That is so even if we are talking about human givers and receivers. "How sharper than a serpent's tooth it is," cries Lear, "to have a thankless child!" (*King Lear*, 1.4.290–291). But it is a strange serpentine tooth whose most deadly bite afflicts the serpent. You cannot be ungrateful without immediate harm to yourself, and in the depths of your being. Macbeth's humanity begins to unravel from the point when he determines not to accept King Duncan's gifts to him, including his elevation to the earldom of Cawdor, as gifts, but rather as stepping stones to his ambition. "I dare do all that may become a man," he says to his wife, perhaps wishing to be persuaded otherwise. "Who dares do more is none" (*Macbeth*, 1.7.46–47). His words are true. He must become less than a man to do more than it becomes a man to do. The ingratitude unmakes him, dehumanizes him. If that is so in the case of an earl and a king, it is infinitely more so in the case of man and God, as man owes all to God: his life, his nature, his very existence.

And What Have We Gotten for the Price?

In *The Everlasting Man*, G. K. Chesterton noted that the first thing that happened after the Greeks began to worship the natural as if it were divine was that they began also to sink into the unnatural: "Let any lad who has had the luck to grow up sane and simple in his daydreams of love hear for the first time of the cult of Ganymede; he will not be merely shocked but sickened" ("The End of the World"). And indeed now we have parents conniving at spaying and gelding their own children, in the quest of a supposedly "authentic" self, which the child alone knows, when the wisest men the world has ever seen will only with great trembling affirm that they know themselves. Was this a boon, for losing God, that we would lose our reason to boot? C. S. Lewis puts it this way, echoing the words of Jesus, that if you seek first the Kingdom of God and His righteousness, you will get earth in the bargain (Matt. 6:33), but if you seek first for earthly goods, you will lose both: "Aim at Heaven and you will get earth 'thrown in': aim at earth and you will get neither" (*Mere Christianity,* Christian Behavior, "Hope"). Or, as Jesus says, in mysterious and dreadful words, "From him who has not, even what he has will be taken away" (Mark 4:25).

Man does not merely happen to be on a journey. It is his essential nature to be *on the way: homo viator.* As soon as he rests content with what is less than the ultimate glory of God, he begins to lose his very humanity. He fixes a ceiling over his head. Dante had the happy idea of setting Purgatory as a mountain-island surrounded by the waters of the great western ocean, exactly opposite the globe to Calvary in latitude and longitude (*Purgatorio,* 4.76–84). The souls in Purgatory strive ever upward, and as they are purged of one capital vice after another, they climb the mountain, and they find the climbing easier as they go. The mountain's cone points toward Heaven, toward what is beyond man—as all things truly human must do, lest they sink back into the brute beast, or into inanimate matter.

By contrast, consider the plight of the souls in Hell, to whom Charon the ferryman cries as they gather on the dismal banks of the Acheron: *Non isperate mai veder lo cielo*—"Give up all hope to look upon the skies!" (*Inferno,* 3.85). It is not just that they will never enter Heaven. For the Heaven where God dwells is not the sky above us. That sky, that corporeal heaven, says Augustine, we may as well call "earth," since it is but part of the physical universe that

God made (*Confessions*, 10.2). And when Dante the pilgrim attains
to the ultimate heavenly sphere, his guide Beatrice tells him that
it has no location at all, other than in the mind of God (*Paradiso*,
29.109–110). Therefore it is most real, because it suffers no shadow
of change; it circumscribes all the lower spheres; it is circumscribed
by none of them, but it is circumscribed, existentially, intellectually,
by God (114). No, the souls who are damned will never enter there.
But Charon's words express in a frank and claustrophobic way what
that means. They will never again see a sky at all, not even the earthly
sky above us. They will never again see a single star.

What will they see? Nothing but the cramped space of their
own past and their sins. So says the materialist heretic Farinata,
when Dante asks him why the damned seem able to glimpse a little
of the future but nothing of the present. It is because the glory of
Heaven shines a weak light upon them, but when things draw near,
they lose that light, and awareness of the events fades from their
consciousness. "Now you can understand that evermore," says he,
that "dead will be all our knowledge from the time / the future ends,
and judgment shuts the door" (*Inferno*, 10.106–108). At that time,
Dante's guide Virgil has said to him, the lids that are now leaning
against the open tombs of the heretics will be leaning there no more:

> These will be bolted on the day of doom
> when from the Valley of Jehosophat
> the souls bring back their bodies to the tomb.
> (10.10–12)

And that may well stand for all the souls who have lost God: their
destiny is a blank slab of stone above their heads, to seal their tombs.
No Heaven, not even a star, not this blue sky and its lovely clouds;
nothing but matter, and matter, in the end, without the spirit of God
that indwells the world and gives it life and meaning, is a dead end.

How many have been the substitutes we have attempted to set upon the throne of God, how many the destinations that were to fulfill our hearts! We can go to Mars someday, perhaps, and we will find it to be but another earth. "We flee ourselves, whom we can never flee." Did someone in Scripture say that? Lucretius the materialist philosopher and poet said it (*On the Nature of Things*, 3.1065), and he was right to say it, though he did not draw the right conclusion, or I should say that he was never offered the right conclusion to draw. We trade the gold of the true and only Heaven, the one that God offers to us if we would raise our hearts to Him in love, and we get dust in return. Does it matter what color the dust is, or where it came from? "What's this flesh?" says the cynical Bosola, at the moral crisis in John Webster's *The Duchess of Malfi*. "A little crudded milk, fantastical puff-paste ... weaker than those paper prisons boys make to keep flies in; more contemptible, since ours is to preserve earthworms" (4.2).

Dust is dust, and everything roundabout us is dust, unless we see it in the light of the God who made us not for dust but for Himself.

THE SECOND LIE

There Is No Objective Moral Truth

"If God does not exist," says Ivan Karamazov, an atheist with a nagging conscience about his unbelief, "then all things are possible." It is a dreadful saying, and it will come back to bite him, because his half-brother, the bastard Smerdyakov—the moniker suggests a *stench*, fitting for Smerdyakov, as he was begotten by Ivan's father upon an idiot beggar girl called Stinking Lizaveta—overhears him and derives from it the fit conclusion. Smerdyakov kills old Karamazov, his and Ivan's father, and insists that it was with Ivan's approval and even collusion.

I am well aware, again, that people who do not believe in God often do believe in moral laws. They are not all like Smerdyakov, in Dostoyevsky's *The Brothers Karamazov*, or like the energetically malignant Peter Verkhovensky, in *The Devils*, who aims to employ the promised suicide of an associate to advance his socialist cause. Why, they may even believe in unchanging moral laws. But I deny that they have any good warrant to believe in such. And then those same moral laws begin to trickle through their fingers, like water. It is hard to see something disappearing; evanescence is hard to grab hold of; we not only forget, but we forget that we have forgotten. So it is with the evanescence of our sense of moral truth.

Modal Auxiliaries

I will begin by examining what we mean by the modal auxiliary *shall.*

It clearly does not denote something that already exists. Or does it? I am fond of how an Old English list of proverbs begins: *Cyning sceal rice healdan*— "A king shall govern a kingdom" (*Maxims II*). In one sense, the maxim merely describes what anyone can see, just as the same poet says, later on, *Fisc sceal on waetere / cynren cennan*— "In the water a fish / shall know its kind" (28–29). That is simply what fish do. So the maxim is either a tautology or a matter of ordinary observation and common sense. But the word *shall* cannot be so easily trammeled up. Even the king, after all, is not just a king because he rules his realm; rather, because he is a king, he *should* rule his realm. The poet attributes the same kind of moral obligation to men who are not kings: *Til sceal on ethle / domes wyrcean*— "A good man in his native land / shall give judgments" (21–22).

Shall is the crucial word throughout the poem, and if we assume that the poet knew quite well what he was doing, we can take its range of meanings in two ways. One is that the poet has set his moral adjurations amid his natural observations, so that, with considerable ironic force, he can urge us to do the right things just as fish swim in water and birds fly in the air above. The other is that he sees the moral laws as fundamental, observable, actually existent; just as fish swim, so too

> *Geongne aetheling sceolan   gode gesithas*
> *byldan to beaduwe   and to beahgife.*

Good companions must raise   the young lord
to fight on the field   and to give rings for reward.
(15–16)

Let us not have any snobbishness here. If you dismiss the Anglo-Saxon scribe, because he was a riddler in a world of intellectual mists and twilight, you dismiss Confucius, too, in the bright noon of ancient Chinese civilization: "At home, a young man should show the qualities of a son; abroad, those of a younger brother. He should be circumspect but truthful. He should have charity in his heart for all men, but associate only with the virtuous" (*The Sayings of Confucius* [trans. Lionel Giles, 1910], 53). The expression of the virtues—courage, duty, beneficence—will differ from place to place, according as the circumstances and the exigencies of life give them their form, but in their essence they remain shiningly themselves, like gems. Confucius and the Anglo-Saxon scribe would understand one another. We are the ones they would find hard to understand.

How do you cross that strait from what the poet sees fish and birds doing, and bears, boars, trees, mists, clouds, the wind, and the sunshine, and what a good man does? The poet would deny that there is any strait to cross. He would appeal to nature, as would Confucius, or Lao-Tzu, or the ancient Stoics. It is no good objection to say that such an appeal is general rather than specific, since the difficulty is seldom in recognizing the general principles of moral truth. How we should be is one thing; what that means we must do, here, now, is another. But to deny absolute moral truth is to deny that there is any meaning to claims as to *how we should be*, quite apart from circumstances. I will deal later with attempts by moralizing amoralists to save the modal *should*. For now, I note that the Anglo-Saxon poet sees God at work in both the way natural things are and the way rational, freely choosing persons should be:

> *Tungol sceal on heofenum,*
> *beorhte scinan,   swa him bebead Meotud.*

> A star in the sky
> Shall shine out bright   as God bade it to do.
>   (49–50)

We must not think here that God issues a command that is extrinsic to the star, compelling it to behave as it does. God made the star and the law it abides by; stars shine because that is what stars do, and there are stars because God made them. Good men are good because they do what good men do—and yes, I know that there is a circle here we must deal with; good men do the bidding of God, who made them such as to thrive upon goodness, as men are made in the image of God. The moral commands of God are not to be considered as extrinsic to our nature, applied from without, as if God might give a kick to a star. The laws the stars obey are themselves created by God; if you set aside the matter, we may say that there is no distinction between star and stellar law.

On What Compulsion?

Why *should* we love our fellow man, who so often is not lovable, and who sometimes is poison to us? Let us turn to the greatest literary genius who ever lived, who saw most deeply into the strange caverns of the human heart. I speak of Shakespeare, of course; and here, of his play *The Merchant of Venice*.

Portia, disguised as a young lawyer, has reviewed the bond that the moneylender Shylock has drawn up with his enemy Antonio. The latter has a few habits that would now make us blanch. He has been in the habit of kicking the Jew, spitting on him, and calling him a mongrel. He is not entirely without reason there. Shylock has preyed upon young Christians who spend their money too freely, as young men about town are wont to do, and he charges them interest on the loans they take up, interest great enough to hang them with. But Antonio lends money gratis, says Shylock, growling, because that "brings down / the rate of usance here with us in Venice" (1.3.41–42). And it is Antonio, not Shylock, who is the merchant of Venice for which the play is named. The distinction is significant, since it is the merchant, not the moneylender, who takes extravagant but socially productive risks, setting so many of his goods at sea, where they may fall into the hands of pirates, or go to ruin in a storm, or fail just short of delivery if the ship smashes against the rocks of the land to which it is sailing. It is Antonio, not Shylock, who must also depend upon a great network of laws and customs that keep people honest. For there were no telephones and computers in those days, and news about his goods could come to him only after much time had passed, assuming that the reports were reliable. The system of international trade and banking wherein Antonio acts is enforced not so much by armies or by court rulings that a determined person could not escape, but by a common and internal acceptance of what is right and wrong, regardless of its immediate benefit to yourself. That included a network of "factors" — that is, agents, who if they had a mind to do it could rob you blind.

In any case, Portia has concluded that the terms of the bond are forfeit and that, by the law of Venice, Shylock has the right to cut off a pound of Antonio's flesh, where and how he pleases. Let us stipulate that Shylock considers himself a law-abiding man and that, despite his angling for Antonio's life, he has never intentionally violated a single law of Venice (nor has Antonio, for that matter), and he never would. He is righteous, if righteousness consists in hewing to written law. He calls his house "sober" (2.5.36), though for his daughter Jessica it is "hell" (2.4.2), because its characteristic is neither love nor goodness but a narrow legalism. He is glad to hear that the bond is as he has planned, but then Portia attempts to get him to see something aside from the bond.

"Then must the Jew be merciful," she says.

"On what compulsion must I? Tell me that," says Shylock (4.1.181–182).

On what compulsion?

I will return to this scene shortly. In the meantime, I suggest that when it comes to acknowledging the moral law, man has only a few intellectual alternatives.

First, he may deny that there is any such.

What happens then? You have anarchy, or mass compulsion. Men are fit for self-government to the degree that they restrain their passions and direct them aright, but if they do not acknowledge that *right* has any stable meaning, they will find reasons to do what they wish to do, and who will gainsay them? One man's theft is another man's redistribution of income. One man's adultery is another man's liberation of repressed sexual desire. One man's vandalism is another man's artistic expression of protest or rebellion.

Obviously, we cannot live this way. Civilization depends upon our taking countless things for granted: for example, that the cars in the oncoming lane will stay on their side of the road. When I was a boy, we all took for granted that people would not steal your car, and that is why we often left the keys there, for convenience. Children had the run of the town because we all took for granted that no one would hurt them. Acknowledgment of the moral law sets people free.

But where the moral law is not acknowledged as law, the steps beneath you begin to give, the cables on the elevator begin to fray, the policeman looks less like a friend than like a mercenary soldier from a foreign land, and every home your child may visit is a possible bordello or house of horrors. Trust is gone. It is Hobbes's war of all against all, where the life of man is, in his famous phrase, "solitary, poor, nasty, brutish, and short" (*Leviathan*, 1.13). Hobbes derived this vision of the "state of nature" not from direct experience of any such, but from the horrible collapse of law and common decency occasioned by the Thirty Years' War, and, on the literary or imaginative side, from the speculations by the ancient poet Lucretius, on what prehistoric and pre-civilized man was like. Men, said Lucretius, entered into a common pact not to harm one another, while keeping the women and children safe, as was just (*On the Nature of Things*, 5.1020). Later, they discovered the arts of war, and every man's hand was against every other, until

> some men showed how to make magistrates
> And appoint courts — for they would live by laws.
> Weary of living by brute force, exhausted
> From lack of friendship, men, of their own will, fell
> The sooner under the strict laws and the courts.
> (5.1140–1144)

These, for Lucretius, were effective not because they enacted the moral law but because of the fear of punishment. We have simply shifted force from the individual to the state, which then assumes the prerogative to prescribe what shall be "moral" and what not. Hobbes saw the matter quite clearly, though he drew the wrong conclusion. The human condition in his time forbade any merely local pact for mutual immunity. There were too many people doing too many things. It required government on a vast scale, his so-called Leviathan, the state as god, subsuming under its authority all individual wills and organizing them toward common ends. Thus does man purchase his peace at the price of his liberty.

The state works by compulsion. It cannot be otherwise. And yet compulsion must be less and less effective the farther it is from its object, and the more human its object is. Compulsion implies a kind of mechanical action, reducing the agent and the patient to quanta of force and resistance — and indeed it is that kind of universe that Hobbes assumes we live in, as he conceives of human beings as if they were atoms of will and power, thus to be directed or channeled or thwarted or canceled out. Even James Madison retained more than a trace of this mechanical way of thought when he tried to justify the American Constitution on the grounds not that it would bring people into unity, but that it would set one force against an opposite force, frustrating both, like gears moving in such a way as to grind together and come to a halt. Well, I can construct a network of gears, wheels, levers, and arms, to turn a millstone and grind corn to powder. But man resists such reduction. He is beyond any system. Madison, I believe, understood this, and he never suggested that the political mechanism he and the drafters of the Constitution invented *must* work, *must* produce justice and promote the common good. It is rather what he thought might give Americans a decent chance at it.

I dearly wish we would keep the distinction in mind. Thus you can do the quasi-mechanical thing, and compel children to go to school, but you cannot compel them to do the human thing, which is to learn. Or if you can compel some measure of learning—holding above their heads the threat of tests—you cannot compel the love of learning, because love, by its very nature, cannot be compelled but can only be given in freedom. The state, acting by means of compulsions, must fail at tasks that are supposed to engender love and to be energized by love; we might as easily have state-arranged romance as state-compelled wonder. The state can threaten you with prison if you commit a crime, but the state cannot hold forth for you the wonder of a moral law, unless that same state recognizes that it is inferior to the moral law, and even then, the state is hardly the right agent for what must be eminently personal. The quality of romance or of wonder or of appreciation of the beauty of the moral law, we might say, taking our cue from Portia, "is not strained" — that is, not a matter of constraint, of force. The attempt to force a human flourishing must fail. But the failure provides the state with a cause to attempt more, ever more, at greater expense, and with more intrusive meddling into affairs that do not belong in its purview. What was once an initial and relatively benign act of compulsion, requiring citizens to send their children to school until a certain age, is now a vast and incomprehensible tangle of compulsions, mandating what must be in the textbooks, what must be the attitude of teachers toward incipient sexual perversion in their students, what must be the relative numbers of boys and girls in team sports, what certificates the teachers must have and how they must have procured them, and on and on.

The schools preach, in these regards, what redounds to the power of the schools, an incoherent combination of moral relativism, since it is supposed to be offensive to say that this or that action (usually sexual) is wrong, and a compelled obeisance to those current social fads that make people moral weaklings and thus more dependent upon the state. One of the bitterly ironic results is a kind of segregation that people in once Christian nations never knew before. In one group, we find people who still uphold objective moral truth, or whose circumstances and whose natural endowments make it possible or profitable for them to restrain their lust and wrath. These people hold to something like moral decency, and so they can negotiate their way in this world of compulsions. In the other group, we find the morally confused, or those whose natural bent is toward lust and wrath, whose energies are unruly and in need of much instruction and discipline. These will fall more and more readily and terribly into chaos. The college graduate whose head is filled with feminism is not the most dreadful victim of its destructive effects. She lives well, though under the state compulsions she tamely accepts. But her sisters who more urgently need the moral law, and who more urgently need the strength of intact family life, do not live so well. And they live in very different places. The misfortune — a failure largely engineered by the state — causes her and others who see only the local effects of action and not its premises or its long-range or broadly extended effects to urge the state to do more, making matters worse, until even that last thread of liberty is gone, and, as the poet Sidney says about an adulterous desire that can go nowhere good, "like slave-born Muscovite, / I call it praise to suffer tyranny" (*Astrophil and Stella*, 2.10–11).

I might add, too, that an acknowledged moral law both tends to restrain the state and to ground what it does in what its citizens readily accept. Thus, a state that taxes me in order to dredge a harbor, because we all readily accept that trade is good, is less of a tyrant than is the state that taxes me in order to finance an army not to protect my nation but to promote, in the world, "democratic values" that are vague and dubious and often incompatible with the cultures these values would alter or vitiate or destroy. Moral duties give way and are replaced with political objectives, and with greater and broader assumption of power. Deny the moral law, and even if you do restrain yourself—because you have good taste, perhaps, or because of good habits whose foundations you do not care to examine—you will end up less a citizen than a functionary, a tool, an object, a cog in a machine, a slave.

The Practical Man

The second possibility is that man will reduce the moral law to pragmatics. The general name for this is utilitarianism, but it, too, has been around since the days of Epicurus and his followers. Epicurus believed that the main object in life was to avoid pain and to pursue pleasure. Since he valued peace of soul and the pleasures of the mind more than pleasures of the body, he preferred sexual licentiousness to romantic monogamy—as did his most renowned and intelligent promoter, the Roman poet Lucretius. If you must have sexual release, says the latter, you'd best procure it by a quick night with a whore, rather than make yourself miserable with love. You should "stroll after a street-strolling trollop and cure yourself," for sex without love is better, as "the goods come without penalty" (*On the Nature of Things*, 4.1062, 1065).

It is hard to see how you can build upon these premises a moral system fit for free people, because of the vast array of things that please some and do not please others, things that are often incompatible with one another and that involve goods that are incommensurate. Into every utilitarian system we must smuggle some objective morality, and then we must rack our brains to figure out how to justify the smuggled goods according to strictly utilitarian requirements, *ex post furto*—after the fact, *after the theft*. Let us grant, for example, that it is a good thing for a little child to have a teddy bear. In fact, it is a billion times greater good that a billion children should each have a teddy bear. But if you could procure that vast good by means of torturing a single human being, you would not do so—even if the torture would not result in permanent injury. It will not do to say that you reject the principle of torture, since, in a utilitarian system, nothing can be rejected on principle, and it must often be the case that individual persons will be required to suffer or to give up some good thing or to deny themselves some pleasure to secure the greatest good for the greatest number. Nor will it do, simply, to say that allowing torture in this case sets an evil precedent for the society, since no claim is made that the torture is good; it is presumably bad, but the bad is outweighed in this instance by the greater good of the billion teddy bears. The precedent—that what we would call an objectively evil action may be justified by its circumstantial results as we imagine them or as they really may be—is already a part of the utilitarian makeup.

The fantasy writer Ursula Le Guin illustrated the point in her short story "The Ones Who Walk Away from Omelas." She imagines a perfect paradise of hedonism and kindness, where men and women offer themselves up sexually to other people, of either sex, like souffles, and where there is no suffering, and no war, and when you want to die, or when you grow ill and death is near, there will always be a pill available to make the transition painless and smooth. But it turns out that all this delight depends upon one child, who must be kept in filth and misery to make it possible. Everyone in Omelas, once they are of age, must go to behold the child upon whose agony they depend. It is supposed to deepen their appreciation of what they have, but, says Le Guin, they are a lesser sort, less wise, than those who walk away and leave that hedonistic paradise behind. I do not know whether Le Guin saw it this way, but I believe that the child must always be an irritant in the utilitarian world. The child is of no immediate economic use. If he is crippled in mind or body, he is a constant and inevitable drain. "Three generations of imbeciles are enough," wrote the utilitarian Supreme Court justice Oliver Wendell Holmes Jr., in his majority opinion in Buck v. Bell (1927), granting the government the power to demand the sterilization of feeble-minded people *against their will*. We should do well to keep in mind the saying of Christ, which turns all such systems on their head, that *unless* we become as little children, we shall not enter the Kingdom of God (Matt. 18:3).

How then to save a decent society, while not believing in the real existence of moral law? We may do what philosophers such as John Rawls do, and retreat a step, imagining what never has existed, that human beings, before any society, blindfolded as to their own individual gain or loss, should come together to establish the rules of the social game, rules that would be fair to everyone and that would result in, again, the greatest good for the greatest number. Aside from the fact that human customs proceed by slow trial and error, what is going on here again is a smuggling, a backdoor attempt to have a moral law while not acknowledging that it exists. For why should we be "fair"? Suppose that *unfairness*, a frank pursuit of power, is likelier to result in glorious achievements, such as those of ancient Rome? All depends on how you rate what is good or bad. Ancient Rome's pile drivers, we may say, were oiled with the blood of slaves. It is not clear to me how the utilitarian, who often desires to deny the objective moral law in order to keep fast his grip on atheism, can compel us to agree, on his own very limited terms, that a pleasant English countryside with a lot of cows and sheep is more to be desired than the heady, brilliant, cruel, and magnificent circuses and arenas of old Rome.

The most direct way — not the most important way, or the best way — to argue utilitarianism down is on its own terms, to show that it is a performative self-contradiction, a disutility to the people who accept it. Consider the ordinary human being. The words of the oracle at Delphi apply to him: "Know thyself." That is because he does not know himself. He does not know what he wants, or what he loves, let alone what he ought to want or love. He is an utterly unreliable judge in his own case. If he is a scrupulous man, he holds himself to impossible standards, and people often cheat him, taking advantage of his uneasy conscience, while less scrupulous people simply forge ahead and do as they please. But the ordinary person does not see himself and his motives. "How can you say to your brother," says Jesus, "'Let me take the speck out of your eye,' when there is a log in your own eye?" (Matt. 7:4). Such people are hypocrites, says Jesus, and the word means something a little different from what we suppose. They, we, are playactors. They, we, are the stars in a drama of the self.

And the star can always find a good reason for what he does, even if "good" and "bad" are taken to refer to what he is content to believe are the probable results, and not the inherent goodness or evil of an action. This is one reason why good intentions pave the road to Hell. When we are justifying what we want to do, looking to its consequences rather than to its inner character, we heap rosy predictions one atop the other; what is merely possible becomes probable, what is probable becomes certain, and even impossibilities, or things only theoretically possible but unexampled in the history of man, become not only possible but desirable, and the very outlandishness of the aim becomes another justification, because we suppose it to be so grand. "I dream of things that never were," said George Bernard Shaw, perhaps while he was preoccupied with justifying the Soviet Union, the most oppressive and inhuman regime ever to burden the earth, at least until Mao Tse-Tung did Stalin one better, "and ask why not." Note that Shaw was patting himself on the back while he said so, and glorying in his perspicacity.

In his autobiography, *Chronicles of Wasted Time*, Malcolm Muggeridge recalled the day, August 23, 1939, when the Molotov-Ribbentrop Pact was concluded, leaving the Soviet Union and Nazi Germany as allies in carving up Europe. Of course, the secular left had long protested loudly that there was nothing in common, no, nothing, between the two evil states. Muggeridge, who saw through man's ideological prancing and preening, understood it otherwise:

> In a way, I had been expecting such a development; never losing an opportunity to say that Bolshevism and National Socialism were the same thing, except that one was a Slav version and the other Teutonic. Why should they not come together, then? My first reaction to the actual line-up between them was a fearful joy. I thought with glee of the confusion in the office of the Daily Worker, where they had to get out a leader saying that the holy war

against Hitler they had been demanding so vociferously must now be regarded as an imperialist one, and at all costs prevented from happening. Of the distress in Cross Street, Bouverie Street and Long Acre, that there should now be so mighty a hole in the common front against Fascism they had been advocating. (*The Infernal Grove*, "The Iron Gates," 344–345)

Distress? They turned on a dime. Muggeridge himself, thinking it over for a moment, knew that they would. It was Muggeridge, after all, who had reported in 1933 about the disaster, the mass starvation, the sheer wastage of knowledge, talent, and cultural capital that was the collectivization of farms in the Ukraine. Millions of people would die, and those who dared to speak out against the experiment, if they were not executed, would be sent off to live out their miserable lives as political prisoners in the gulags far away. Would his report change the minds of the ideologues? Hardly. Muggeridge knew that his reports would cost him his job, as indeed they did. What could the true believers say? There will always be some reason why such a thing can go wrong. When failure stares him in the face, some combination of bad luck and ill will in opponents will sound plausible to any utilitarian who judges his actions by his intentions as to results and not by an inherent good or evil nature in the action. Or he may defer to a vague future time the point at which we should determine its success or failure, and thus instead of doubting his premises and even the purity of his intentions, he demands more and more time, more and more money, more and more flexibility in the moral senses of other people, precisely because of the failure. American schools work this way; that is, it is how they grow more and more ambitious, unaccountable, and monstrous with each manifest failure. If feminism tends to make young women miserable, impatient with their own sex and ungrateful for the other, then what we need is more of the same, more and more. No failure will teach you, if you have all the time in the world and a lot of money.

Judging the Tree

"You will know them by their fruits," said Jesus. "A sound tree cannot bear evil fruit, nor can a bad tree bear good fruit" (Matt. 7:16, 18). The Pharisee Gamaliel, arguing among the Jewish elders as to what they should do with the new sect of Jews who were following Christ, seems to recommend the same course of action and the same criterion for judgment. "Keep away from these men and let them alone," he said. "If this plan or this undertaking is of men, it will fail; but if it is of God, you will not be able to overthrow them" (Acts 5:38–39).

Are they urging upon us a utilitarian view of good and evil?

Not at all. The tree is good not on account of the fruit it produces, and the new belief in Christ will be from God not because it cannot be overcome. The causality works in the other direction. Because the tree is already good, it brings forth good fruit, and if the new belief is from God, it will not be overcome. The order of being proceeds from inherent good to good actions and good results, though the order of judgment *can sometimes* proceed from results to their source or originator. Jesus does not, after all, say that the *only* way to judge a tree is by the fruit you happen right now to perceive, nor does Gamaliel come close to suggesting that the will of God depends upon results, or that what comes from God must always be manifest as such in a clear and immediate way. After all, as he well knew, the Jews had often been persecuted, their great city had been destroyed, and they had been dragged off to captivity in Babylon.

But let us look at this matter closely. Lurking in the shadows of every utilitarian scheme are assumptions about what is good and evil per se and not by circumstance or by their use. John Stuart Mill could only attempt to save utilitarianism by a hierarchical ranking of pleasures, elevating, as Epicurus himself did, the pleasures of the mind above the pleasures of the body. Now, we can always find plausible reasons to do so. The mind reaches further than the body. The mind is of broader development than the body. The mind and not the body is what separates us from the beasts. But it is by no means clear that we are obligated to prefer the mind to the body. Aristippus (ca. 435–356 BC), the hedonistic follower of Socrates, seemed to do the reverse, and to enjoy it heartily; and though he did not recommend to his followers the heady pleasures of cruelty, he did seem to be content as a hanger-on of the tyrant Dionysius of Syracuse. So if we want to assert that a painting by Raphael is a greater good than a night of debauchery, appealing to an independent system of rank, we are trying to have our Falernian wine and drink it too. And indeed most people, if they are trained up in a utilitarian rejection of absolute values, will simply not see why they should prefer, so to speak, clear water to blood.

But it is nevertheless true that evil principles work themselves out in evil actions and disastrous results, though these may be hidden for a time by wealth and power, as they are right now, I believe, in the United States. And it is true that good principles bring forth good actions and health, though again these may be hidden for a time, and from the eyes of poor discerners of things, by poverty and political powerlessness, as they were for many ancient Christians in the Roman Empire before Constantine. We can often employ an order of judgment that proceeds from evident results back toward principles and being, not simply to judge by results, and not only to conjecture that a thing must have been good or bad from the start, but to begin to see *why it was so*. And when we do that, we depart from utilitarianism entirely.

We can derive a clue, ironically enough, from Lucretius himself. The atomist declares that when your principles are incorrect, you will be like someone trying to build a house with a carpenter's square that is not square, a plumb line that doesn't hang straight down, and a straightedge that is not straight. Small errors in principles result in terrible errors in results. The roof sags, the walls buckle, the floors tilt. But that is because the principles were in themselves *wrong* (*On the Nature of Things*, 4.513–521).

The English word *wrong* is most suggestive. It belongs to a large category of words, from the single Indo-European root *wer-*, that have to do with turning and twisting: wring, wrest, wrap, warp, wire, writhe, wrinkle, wry, wrath (for the contorted face of an angry man), wreck, wrist, and so forth. What is crooked will cave in. A hunchbacked man cannot walk upright. Moral wrong is like a warped beam, a tilted wall. Your house may not fall tomorrow. But its very principles are twisted toward failure and destruction.

Suppose we say that the principle of feminism is radically individualist without most feminists themselves acknowledging it to be so, since it posits that the good of each sex is severable from the good of the other, and thus it supplants the household as the fundamental unit of society, setting the individual in its place. Early feminists such as Charlotte Perkins Gilman, in *Herland*, could imagine flowery feminist utopias in which men and women would love each other all the more for there being no appreciable difference between them, and for there being no dependence of one upon the other for anything. It is hard to fathom how anyone could really believe that it would be so. Eros, says Plato, had an ambiguous parentage, born of both Plenty and Penury (*Symposium*, 178), and though he was not thinking of the relations between men and women, he might as well have been, since the sexes are made *for one another* precisely because of their *inequalities*, their differences. Man can never bear or suckle a child; and woman, no matter for the exceptional amazon here or there, could never have begun to build all the vast network of structures we take for granted around us, whose building required not only the full strength of healthy grown men but also a high tolerance for risk, for placing oneself in the way of harm or death. Nor would it have occurred to women to try it. A woman will do much in the immediate case when her child is directly threatened, but otherwise she will do all she can to protect herself and her child from danger. And it is right and good for her to do so.

It follows that any social system or principle that denies either the stark differences between man and woman or their urgent interdependence is built upon falsehood. The principle is *wrong*, like the bent post or the bowed lintel. It cannot support the house. It has not supported the house. Not even feminists now claim that men and women love one another better than ever before, or that households are stronger and children more secure. When the house falls in, some people will draw the reasonable conclusion that there was something wrong with its fundamental structure, with the rule and the level and the plumb line used to build it, or with the materials—not stone but sand. Most people in our time, protected for a while by our wealth, alas, will say instead that it is a perfectly good thing to live in a shambles. Women raising boys without fathers tend to raise weaklings, some of them turning to other men erotically in their longing for the male affirmation that should have come to them naturally, from their fathers. Many such women, unmoved by the wholly unnecessary confusion and suffering, will prefer to say that it is a positive *good* to have raised a man who is no man, and will congratulate themselves for it. But people who retain some sense of right and wrong must be led to reexamine the principles, the seed, and see the initial and deadly error.

Mass Force

"The secularists have not wrecked divine things," said Chesterton, "but the secularists have wrecked secular things, if that is any comfort to them" (*Orthodoxy*, "The Romance of Orthodoxy"). In feverishly attempting to disprove divine agency, they have denied that there is any such thing as human agency, lest the existence of a genuinely free will might lead anyone to conclude that there must be more in the world than the determinism of billiard balls knocking against each other. They do not destroy orthodoxy, he says, but they do "destroy political courage and common sense." The fact is, people will either lapse into despair or they will turn to something, anything, to believe in, to place their hope. The *anything* in question will rarely be the invention of the person himself. For a faith in God, or a belief in and a conscious adherence to an objective moral order, can give a man the strength to resist the pull of mass action, which even if it is not madness incarnate is at least suspect, as being not the flowers and the fruit of a healthy culture, but the output of its quasi-mechanical simulacrum, the mass state, or, to use Gabriel Marcel's oxymoronic label, "mass society." I call it an oxymoron because insofar as a society is characterized by facelessness, by sheer numbers, by a conformity that levels distinctions between place and place, and that tends to obliterate memory—a society such as ours in the United States is now—it is no society at all, but a thing for which we have yet to invent a name, just as the agglutination of human beings dwelling within certain geographical boundaries is not, thereby, a nation, but a something else again, something for which we have no name. And such a thing, a non-society, is dangerous, says Marcel, as it lends itself to the impersonal, and the impersonal makes all kinds of wickedness practicable. It is also opposed to the universal, to the call of intelligence and love. "The masses exist and develop," he says, "only at a level far below that at which intelligence and love are possible" (*Man Against Mass Society*, preface, 10). He is not talking about the working class. He is talking about us all and the way we live, to the extent that we receive instruction and direction from the mechanisms of mass society. That would be a dull thing indeed, except that propaganda comes into play to jolt us into a false sense of morality and a false life, and so the masses are "the stuff of which fanaticism is made."

It is not so hard to see how the mass machine works: by various arms of punitive or seductive compulsion, namely schools, the entertainment industry, mass media, and all entities that can exert power by the sheer force of repetition, relentless, almost unconscious, like items of production on a conveyor belt. How many are the things we must now believe, if we are to be considered good people! That a man may become a woman, or a woman a man, merely by saying so; that a child in the womb is a child if the mother believes it to be so, but a mere clump of cells if not; that the world is going to fry in its self-made hell unless we *Do Something*, something that may impoverish countless people dependent upon gasoline and oil for everyday necessities; that the most important thing in life is to follow your dreams and be yourself and achieve greatness and glory and a house far bigger than you can afford or than anyone actually needs; that schoolteachers and not parents are the best judges, perhaps the only right judges of what a child should learn and how; that medical care is best left to the centralized state; that you cannot be free unless you may indulge any sexual appetite you have, so long as you get the consent of your cooperator in crime; no doubt there are many more I have not time to name. Many of these things are flatly ridiculous. Not the most radical surgeries we have invented, let alone a verbal declaration, can change the sex of a human being. Others are sheer speculations. Sometimes we have a great lot of wishful hoping, which often results in hoping for disaster, so that, for example, if a report comes out that suggests that the earth's warming is not severe and probably not harmful to life on the planet, but possibly the reverse, many people will be disappointed, just as many a feminist resents having to hear that her grandmother, who was a traditional woman all the way, was happier than she is, and her husband treated her very well.

Such de-moralized people — I use the word in two senses: they are dispirited and they have been denied knowledge of the moral law that sets men free — feel they have no selves unless they manage to assert them, loudly and with threats that are, in spirit, suicidal or homicidal. Hence it is they, not I, who say that if we deny them their fantastical self-made worlds, we commit "genocide," even as we do not intend to lay a finger on them, so easily do they bruise. All is to proceed according to the dictates of the self, but as Marcel says, "it is *never* from the self that light pours forth," though the ego is always ready to thrust itself forward, for "the ego is essentially pretentious" ("The Universal against the Masses, II").

Now, if you are not going to be rushed downstream by the mass phenomena, you must have a strong principle that is not dependent upon that river, indeed that stands above it and against it in judgment. This something cannot come from the self, because the self is the locus of the problem. We cannot think our way into morality, because we habitually use our minds to justify what we have already chosen to do, nor do we think clearly when our passions are in play, and that problem becomes especially acute when the ubiquitous Image Machine blares and flashes at us, at all times and in all public places. The person most likely to float along passively — though not perhaps quietly and pleasantly — while he prides himself on his independence, is he for whom the following words make no sense: "This kind of action is evil, regardless of how good it feels to you, regardless of what everyone is saying about it, and regardless of what you project, conveniently enough, to be its likely results. It is simply *wrong*, and no circumstances and no pressure of popular opinion can make it right." Thus it is that you can have, in the same person, someone who says that all moral views are "socially constructed" and therefore relative and subjective, and someone who is utterly intolerant if anyone should show signs of veering *from* where the force of the mass phenomena is driving the preponderant majority of his fellow citizens. And we should be quite clear about whose wallets will fatten from it. As Chesterton says, "The *rules* of a club are occasionally in favor of the poor member. The drift of a club is always in favor of the rich one."

No one, I guess, would say, consciously, that he wishes to be formed wholly by the vagaries of mass media and entertainment and schooling, and that his childhood ambition is to make rich people richer thereby. Yet that must needs happen if he relinquishes his hold on objective moral truth. He will be carried along. He has, after all, no objective aim, and whatever aim he may have that is somewhat counter to where the river is going he will have no strength to attain. To see why, let us return to Portia and Shylock.

Not Compulsion, but Love

When Shylock asks Portia why he *must* be merciful, he is thinking in terms of statutory law. He knows he has that in his favor. According to the laws of Venice, his bond is good, and Antonio must give up that pound of flesh, which Shylock plans to carve out of him nearest the heart. Of course, we are here in a realm close to the fairy tale, but that is not the point. We must give the dramatist his imaginative world because he wants to show us something about law and justice, mercy and love, that applies not simply to the Venice of his fancy but to all human communities.

Just here, the attempt to reduce the moral law to what happens to be the positive law for a certain place and time collapses. It was no excuse for the men at the Nuremberg trials to say that they were merely following the law. They were guilty of crimes against humanity because the moral law, absolute and universal, stood in judgment over and against the law of the National Socialists, and it was that law they were to follow, even at risk of their lives; at the least, they were not to do all they could to promote the unlawful regime. What Shylock is attempting to do is evil. Nor can he claim as an excuse that Antonio has done offensive things to him. He is seeking the life of a good man; he is seeking the life of his fellow traveler on the way to the grave.

People who do not hold to moral absolutes will find ways to work within the bounds of statutory law, like termites, to do as they please, and they will find the reasons too, never far to seek. You may say to them that if everyone behaved as they do, the social order would fall apart. They may then reply that that is not the business of the individual but of the state. You may try to rescue the moral law as Immanuel Kant does in his *Groundwork for the Metaphysics of Morals*, by a double move. You say that the determining feature of man is reason, and you note that reason is of universal application, nor is it dependent on the vagaries and the errors of empirical investigation. Therefore, when you act, you must act with a reason, what Kant calls a maxim, and this maxim must be independent of the specifics of your feelings, your situation, and what you suppose you may gain from the action. A man, says Kant, must never act in such a way that the principle of his action, the maxim, cannot be made universal without self-contradiction, a violation of reason itself. Thus, if you make a promise knowing full well that you do not intend to keep it, your maxim, if extended to all men, would make it so that promises themselves could never be made, as no one would trust them. You would be sawing off the *rational* limb on which you sit.

But that itself is to reason as a calculator does, and not as a man. The contradiction, if all we are talking about is rational evaluation, does not harm you in the instant deed. You may be sawing off the limb on which some later promise-breaker would be sitting, while you get away with it, and for your purposes that is enough. But even if we can say that it is irrational for you to make a lying promise, it does not follow that you must not make it this once, and it certainly does not follow that you must do more than avoid irrationality in the universal application of the principles of what you do. For to view the moral law as a mere set of prohibitions is to view it as a truant schoolboy might. Nothing in such a view attracts, inspires, moves to action, flourishes forth in glorious and beautiful deeds. Kant can at best suggest to us a bloodless reason for *not acting* according to a rather limited set of false maxims—those he can identify only because, as a human being made of flesh and blood, he possesses already an intuition of the moral truth.

But we want to act, not just to sit still. Hence Portia's reply to Shylock must move us from prohibition to invitation, from the fear of the immediate consequences of lawbreaking to a desire to be kingly and bounteous, all while we know full well how desperate would be our case were God to judge us as severely as the moral law may demand:

> The quality of mercy is not strained;
> It droppeth as the gentle rain from heaven
> Upon the place beneath. It is twice blest;
> It blesseth him that gives and him that takes:
> 'T is mightiest in the mightiest; it becomes
> The throned monarch better than his crown:
> His scepter shows the force of temporal power,
> The attribute to awe and majesty,

Wherein doth sit the dread and fear of kings;
But mercy is above this sceptered sway;
It is enthronèd in the hearts of kings,
It is an attribute to God himself;
And earthly power doth then show likest God's
When mercy seasons justice. Therefore, Jew,
Though justice be thy plea, consider this,
That, in the course of justice, none of us
Should see salvation: we do pray for mercy;
And that same prayer doth teach us all to render
The deeds of mercy.
(4.1.183–201)

Mercy cannot be constrained, without ceasing to be mercy. Our heart's desire is, or ought to be, not merely to avoid doing evil but to approach the good, to embrace it and love it. Mercy thus blesses both the giver and receiver, as it makes the giver resemble more and more closely the throned monarch, and even God Himself. If the psalmist, as he lies upon his bed, meditates upon the law of God, it is not as a set of prohibitions but as a gift, the *dabarim* or utterances of God to His people whom He loves; and it is his love for this incomparable gift that makes the psalmist, as he says, wiser than his teachers (Ps. 119:99).

We see that the problem of good and evil cannot be severed from the problem of the human heart. For as St. Paul says, "the evil we do not want to do, we do anyway, and the good we want, we fail to do" (Rom. 7:15). Our hearts are divided against themselves. Even if we see what the good is, we do not fully desire it, because we are attached to some lower good, or our hearts do not beat warmly enough. Shylock must somehow be moved to desire a greater good than vengeance against his enemy. We do not know what his desires will be. He is hoist with his own petard; the law he depended upon, literally interpreted, just as he has interpreted the letter of his bond with Antonio, will destroy him, unless he begins to acknowledge a good that transcends the statutory law. That is the inner meaning of his being content to become a Christian at the end of the play, rather than to die still railing in anger against his foe. We may not care for the element of compulsion therein, but Shylock is guilty of conspiring against his enemy's life; he is a murderer in intent. From Shakespeare's point of view, the man has been saved from himself and has had a door of mercy opened to him, to eternal life.

It will do us no good to say, with Kant, that a certain class of action is wrong, unless we are moved to reject it, to dislike it, even to loathe it. And what moves man to action, if not a vision of what is beautiful? That is not compulsion, but, we might say, propulsion; not force, but attraction; not fear, but delight. Well did the Greeks see *to kalon*, "the good," as also "the beautiful." These stand or fall together, both in essence and in practical action. But modern man has bought the foolish lie, that there is no such thing as beauty, and as if to ratify the lie, he has managed to tear down or to deface one beautiful church, public building, musical composition, prayer, poem, and human custom after another, and for the most part has not even attempted to replace them. To that lie we now turn.

THE THIRD LIE

There Is No Such Thing as Beauty

> Who says that fictions only and false hair
> Become a verse? Is there in truth no beauty?
> — *George Herbert, "Jordan (I)," 1–2*

> Beauty is truth, truth beauty; that is all
> Ye know on earth, and all ye need to know.
> — *John Keats, "Ode on a Grecian Urn," 49–50*

THE YEAR IS around 1200. You are a glazier, a master of the art, and you are working on the most important side window in the Cathedral of Notre-Dame des Chartres. You have the whole conception in mind. Our Lady—and you do mean both words, you do mean *Lady* and not merely *woman*, and you do mean *our*, because you conceive the relationship to be deeply personal and warm—is to be seated on a throne, and in her bosom is to be the Christ Child, looking straight at the viewer, raising His right hand in blessing, as He holds an open book in His left hand, with the pages facing the beholder. Somehow, you are to make everything about Christ evident in your art, in your deliberate and delicate choices, and here the bishop of the diocese and the canon and some friendly scholars have come to your assistance. You know that the portrayal of Mary here is not as the Mother of Sorrows, but as the Seat of Wisdom, for in her bosom is Christ, as St. Paul says, "the power of God and the wisdom of God" (1 Cor. 1:24). So they have suggested the text you will show in the open book. It is *omnis vallis implebitur*, "every valley shall be filled." Why?

You are wise enough to have a strong sense of it, though you do not read Latin. The words are from Isaiah, from a triumphant and joyful prophecy of renewal, of comfort, of the glorious advent and rulership of the Messiah:

> A voice cries: "In the wilderness prepare the way of the LORD, make straight in the desert a highway for our God. Every valley shall be lifted up, and every mountain and hill be made low; the uneven ground shall become level, and the rough places a plain. And the glory of the LORD shall be revealed, and all flesh shall see it together, for the mouth of the LORD has spoken." (Isa. 40:3–5)

They are, as you know well, the words that John the Baptist used to identify himself and his mission, when the Pharisees from Jerusalem asked him who he was and what he was doing, baptizing people in the Jordan River and calling them to repentance. But John was no marker for himself. He points always to Christ, for there is one coming, he said, "the thong of whose sandal I am not worthy to untie" (John 1:27). How do you portray this Christ, who is a child, but who will walk the road to Calvary, who will die upon the Cross and be raised again on the third day?

These are, as you understand, theological and artistic questions at once. Some of your choices are determined for you, by the artists you have learned from, whose work has entered the minds and souls of Christians for many centuries. So then, the halo about Christ's head must illustrate who He is, and that means that you will see the

Cross in it, the top and the two sides of the crossbeam, suggesting the Trinity, and suggesting not simply that Christ will be crucified but that He is eternally the One who has given Himself up for the sins of the world: "We preach Christ crucified," says St. Paul, and there is no other Christ to preach (1 Cor. 1:23). That is why, though Our Lady's feet are sandaled, you show His hands and His bare feet. Those, you know, will be pierced by the nails. And you do something else. When someone is seated, the folds of his robe will fall, usually a little to one side or another, and so, as if you were doing no more than portraying in glass what anyone might see, you show the robe of Christ settling open a little to His left and the onlooker's right, so that more of Christ's right side will show; and that is the side that will be pierced by the lance.

Our Lady, you say to yourself, must fairly glow with beauty and innocence, but how can you show what she means as the Seat of Wisdom? If you had her looking sternly forward, she would be forbidding, as if her wisdom were unapproachable. And yet this Lady is she to whom you and your fellow Catholics appeal, to pray to Christ on your behalf. If you had her looking down and aside, you might be suggesting that she found her wisdom in herself, in the penetration and the genius of her thoughts. Instead, she looks forward, with a slight tilt of her head, and a slight smile upon her lips, inviting you not so much to look at her as to look at whom she is showing to you, the Christ Child. That look is exactly how a mother, quietly proud of her child, might look, and yet the power of the look is in its transcendent meaning. For Christ does not have that smile on His lips. He looks forward toward the beholder, and slightly upward toward the Father, with a sober set to His mouth. He is the judge, after all. Yet he is a merciful judge, and we can tell it from the fact, a natural thing after all, that His face resembles that of His mother, or, indeed, her face resembles His, since He, her son, is also her Maker.

Hundreds and hundreds of choices do you make! That incomparable pair of blue colors, a rich blue and a light and veil-like blue, for Mary's robes; the five gems that are inlaid in her crown, symmetric, diamond-shaped emeralds at the ends, then oval rubies, then a single diamond-shaped sapphire in the center, all echoed in the tracery at the inner edge of her blue halo; the golden censers on silver chains that swing above her head, and that help to frame her figure, each censer held by an angel in a panel that is both within the composition and without; the deep and comforting emerald green of Christ's halo and of the edging of His inner garment, green the color of hope; the deep red background of Mary's seat, harmonizing and contrasting so well with the inlays of eight-petaled blue flowers that are like the "buttons" where the cloth is gathered in, eight flowers we see, though if Mary were to rise from her seat there would be seven times three, or twenty-one, of them; the white dove, edged with the slightest touches of silvery blue, that is the Holy Spirit descending straight down from Heaven, beak first, upon the throne, with three blue rays of light proceeding symmetrically from a point directly below the eye; it is a veritable fugue of light and color, of motion and stillness, of shape and form.

If someone were to ask you *why* you wanted to make your portrait of Mary and Jesus beautiful, you would likely furrow your brows and wonder whether you had heard the words right. Beauty needs no justification. It would be like asking why someone wants to go outdoors in the sunshine, or why someone enjoys looking at a handsome human face. The question makes no sense. But neither would it make any sense to you, the medieval glazier, if someone said that what you had done was *not itself beautiful*, but only that it happened that people liked to look at it—in fact, were enrapt by it. You would walk away, wondering whether the person was in his right mind, or you might reply that he had gotten things backwards. We do not call it beautiful because people like to look at it. A lot of people in ancient Rome enjoyed seeing a lion tear a victim to shreds in the arena, but they would not have called it beautiful. Rather, because a thing is beautiful, people will be attracted to it, and often *against their other inclinations*. The atheist in the Cathedral of Notre-Dame des Chartres will be attracted by the magnificent beauty of the art, and the soaring harmonies in stone and glass, while feeling vaguely uneasy about it all, as if he did not belong there.

A World in a Grain of Sand

Denen die Gott lieben, muessen alle Dinge zum Besten dienen, reads the stone at the grave of the titan of modern mathematics, Bernhard Riemann: "All things serve for the best to those who love God" (Rom. 8:28). Riemann was a devout man who believed that his mathematical work, which I wager will remain fruitful for a thousand years, was a form of service to God. He worked by allowing himself to be guided by intuitions of beauty and order, discovering or conjecturing a theorem, and afterwards searching for proof. Beauty guided the mind of Riemann's younger contemporary, Georg Cantor, himself also a deeply devout Lutheran. To Cantor, we owe the notion that I have mentioned, that the infinite set of natural numbers (1, 2, 3, and so forth) is of a different order, what Cantor labeled as "aleph-null," from that of the set of real numbers between any two numbers: the "continuum," what Cantor labeled as "aleph-one." Cantor believed that the proof of their difference in order was given to him by God. It roiled the mathematical community because some mathematicians insisted that unless you could provide a specified *example* of what you were proving must exist, it made no sense to assert its existence. I beg your patience again, reader: there is simply no way to specify all the numbers in any continuum, because if you could so specify them individually, we would be talking about a set that would match that of the natural numbers, 1, 2, 3, and so forth. Cantor understood that his beautiful result had profound implications for questions regarding the existence of infinite objects, and even for the existence of God.

Let your guide be beauty, and you will be led into truth. Tradition has it that Pythagoras discovered the mathematical relationships among musical notes, a beautiful result indeed. Cut a string into two lengths, one half as long as the other, and stretch them both tight, securing them at both ends. If the longer string plays C, let us say, the shorter string will play it also, exactly one octave higher. Other mathematical relationships obtain between other pairs of notes. If the shorter string is not half but two-thirds as long as the other, it will play G, the so-called fifth or dominant, to the other's C. We know now that these things happen because sound travels in waves, and if the waves have frequencies such that their crests and troughs often coincide, we will hear the combination as harmonic. It won't be chaotic, like contrary winds lashing the surface of a lake, with the waves splashing against each other—the "noise," the "static," if you will, of disordered water. It will be as if you cast two stones into the lake when it is still, stones of such sizes that the ripples they make will not simply counteract each other but will merge into harmony, increasing their joint power. In any case, the strong relationship between beauty in music and beauty in numbers entered the Western imagination and remained there for almost two millennia, mainly by means of *On the Foundations of Music*, the work of the Christian polymath, Boethius (d. 524), who says that the laws of music are the bridge between geometrical objects that do not change or move and the heavenly bodies that do move. If we spurn the study of music—and by that, Boethius does intend to range from the sounds we hear to the motions of the stars that we cannot hear—we can hardly, he says, be called lovers of wisdom at all.

Thus do we not only see the beautiful; the beautiful enables us to see. "In thy light," says the psalmist, "do we see light" (Ps. 36:9). Let me again take a case from mathematics. We define a prime number as an integer that cannot be divided by any other integer without leaving a remainder. (We leave out of consideration the number 1, which doesn't split any number but leaves it intact.) You can't divide 7 by anything other than 7, and not get a remainder. Thus the first prime numbers are 2, 3, 5, 7, 11, 13, 17, 19, 23, 29, 31, 37, and so on. There are mathematicians who work almost solely on prime numbers, which have strange and usually surprising applications all across mathematics. They are even important in cryptography, for if you multiply two staggeringly large primes, you will get a number that it will be almost impossible for someone else to "crack" into its component parts. Some primes occur in pairs separated by 2, such as 11 and 13, and sometimes these pairs are as close to one another as possible (191, 193, 197, 199). It is conjectured that the number of such pairs is infinite, though the fact has not yet been proved, and I do not know whether we even conjecture that the number of pairs of pairs is infinite.

We do know that the number of primes is infinite, and if you will follow me with a little patience here, I will provide a simple proof. *Suppose it were not so.* Then there must be a *finite* set of N prime numbers, P1, P2, P3, ... PN. All right. Now multiply all those numbers together, and add 1. The result is P1 × P2 × P3 × ... × PN + 1. Call this number Q. Now, it's clear that none of those prime numbers can divide Q without a remainder, namely 1. Therefore either Q is a prime number itself, or Q is the product of prime numbers that are not in that set. Therefore the set of prime numbers is not finite. Therefore it is infinite, and there is no largest prime number.

You can test it a bit. Multiply 2 × 3 × 5 × 7 × 11. That's 2,310. Add 1: 2,311. And as it happens, 2,311 is itself a prime. Multiply

2 × 3 × 5 × 7 × 11 × 13. That's 30,030. Add 1: 30,031. That is not a prime. It is 509 × 59, and those numbers are prime.

There are a lot of things I find lovely in this argument. Unlike the number crunching above, it involves no brute force, only clear reasoning. The reasoning proceeds by orderly steps, and though the result feels inevitable, it still strikes us with a surprise; we may even smile when we see it, and say, "So that's that!" And the reasoning itself, its form, *can be extended to all realms in which there are only two possibilities, each excluding the other.* For either there is a largest prime number, which is the same as saying that the set of primes is finite, or there is not. No third possibility exists. So if you assume that there is not, and that leads you into absurdity or self-contradiction, then the converse *must be true.* It is a powerful tool: it can move the universe itself. For the universe is either the creative work of an intelligent mind, or it is not. No third possibility exists, though if it is the first, it may yet be corrupted or incomplete; those are logically though perhaps not theologically consistent with believing that the universe is a creation and not an accident of chance and happenstance matter and a handful of non-necessary physical laws that govern the matter.

I have heard a great scientist, one who now doubts its validity, say that Darwin's theory of evolution, with natural selection as the sifting device and random mutation as the motor, was beautiful. He did not mean that it pleased his moral sense. He meant that it explained all the wild variety of life around us by appealing to a very small number of commonly observable facts, though the act of imagination that made the leap from fact to theory, from what you see with your eyes to what you see with your mind, was by no means a common thing. Such is the force of evolution as a theory, it has come to dominate the imagination of Western man, so that we take for granted that societies "evolve," casting aside customs and laws that do not work in favor of those that do, while man grows happier and wealthier and wiser with every passing generation. And certainly we cannot say that the theory is *all wrong*, even when we apply it beyond its legitimately scientific bounds. For there is such a thing as trial and error, and if a social custom or a political system is an obvious and colossal failure, even mankind will eventually figure it out and discard it in favor of something else.

I will return shortly to what is *not beautiful* about the theory, simply taken in its aesthetic properties, aside from scientific fact. But it does reveal to us something about beauty. It is *not skin-deep*, and it is not merely in the eye of the beholder. The experience is subjective, no doubt of that. I understand that some of my readers will not be moved by the beauty of my little proof about prime numbers, and so, too, I, who do not know much about soccer, may be unmoved by a foot change worked by a player moving the ball quickly downfield and eluding his opponent. I may see it, I may even acknowledge that it has happened, but I may have no idea of how difficult it is to do, and with what deftness and skill the player has managed it. Just so, people may look at Caravaggio's dramatic painting of the conversion of St. Paul, with the body of an enormous horse taking up half of the canvas, and they may confess that it is striking, but they cannot tell why the horse ought to be there, or what is going on with the old man who leads the horse by the bridle but who does not otherwise seem aware of anything going on, including what has happened to the apostle, who lies on the ground, facing a dark sky, his eyes shut, and his arms flung out wide in shock or terror or vision. I can imagine many a tourist saying, "Well, that's something," and pausing to look at it for a respectable length of time, growing a bit uncomfortable, because he knows he should be more deeply moved than he is, and he wishes he knew more, so that he could enter into the painting's spirit more deeply.

But even if we stand shuddering before the work, stirred to the core, the fact that we experience beauty in this interior way does not mean that there is no objective beauty for us to experience. We do not say that love does not exist, though it is experienced subjectively, and though we are often in a muddle about what love is and whether we are feeling it or are just fooling ourselves. Love does exist; it is an objective fact. The same goes for beauty. There is something there for us to see, to feel striking at the core of our being. The medieval mystic Richard of St. Victor (d. 1173) says that love is an eye: *ubi amor, ibi oculus*. That is the crucial insight animating his discussion of the cognitive power of love (*On the Twelve Patriarchs*, XIII). It is not just that we love what we see but that love itself enables us to see. We look with great eagerness on what we love, that we may know it more deeply, and the more deeply we know it, the more of its beauty we perceive, and the more we love it. Antoine de Saint-Exupéry echoed the Victorine philosopher in that most wonder-stirring of children's books, *The Little Prince*. "Goodbye," says the wise fox to the Little Prince, after they have "tamed" one another and become friends. "Here is my secret. It's very simple. Only by the heart can you see anything well. What's essential is invisible to the eyes" (chap. 21). If you do not love someone, you will never know him to the depths of his being. Beauty is similar. It is not just that we see beauty with our eyes or with the eyes of the mind; beauty enables us to see. That is one of the things we find most enthralling about it, most enchanting: beauty opens the eyes.

It does so, in part, because of its explanatory or exemplary power. Let us turn again to the great window at Chartres. We would not find it so beautiful if it were merely a patchwork of colors without shape and without any representation of objects and persons. We would also not find it so beautiful if it were exactly as it is, but alone, not situated in the cathedral, meaning, ultimately, not situated in the entire story of Christ and of man and his salvation. Each object in the window refers to the others in an intricate network of relationships—in shape, color, significance, and hierarchical order. If you understand why the Christ Child is not looking at His mother but toward us, then you are along the way toward understanding what the entire window is about, the entire wall of windows, the entire cathedral, the entire Christian faith. If you understand why He is a child here, even though He also appears in the pose of the Pantocrator, ruler of the universe, then you are along the way to understanding why Mary has tilted her head in an act of modest submission, and you may begin to touch the deepest ironies of the Christian faith, that unless you become as little children, you shall not enter the Kingdom of Heaven, that the first shall be last and the last shall be first, that the widow with her poor coin gave more to the treasury than all the rich people did put together, and that men who worked with their hands—masons, glaziers, carpenters, painters, sculptors, and lesser lights who built the scaffolds and lit the fires and hauled the stones with pulleys and winches—could be set free to erect the most magnificent building in the world. Beauty is a light, and it enlightens.

The property I am describing admits—*in part*, not as the whole of beauty, not by a long shot—of a mathematical description, called self-similarity. That is, the smallest feature of a thing is structured like larger features, and so on, so that if you have a good look at the small, you will see the great. Thus the little pinnacles that surmount the caps of the buttresses at Notre-Dame de Paris resemble the great spires themselves, and the interlacing ribs that frame the rose windows are like roses in nature, springing up with precise relationships between each round of petals as you move from the center to the circumference. The architects were quite aware of a whole host of ratios to which they attributed profound theological import. Those included but by no means were limited to the so-called Golden Ratio, self-similar all the way down, or all the way in, as you happen to look at it. If you construct a regular pentagon and you connect all the vertices, you will make a five-pointed star with another pentagon inside it. If you connect the vertices of the inner pentagon and extend them so they meet the outer pentagon, and you keep doing the same sort of thing every time you see two points that can be connected with lines parallel to the edges of either of these pentagons, you will make one pentagon after another, whole nests of them embedded about and within one another, and countless triangles—all of the same two shapes, with this unique feature, that in any triangle A cut into two other triangles B and C, the area of the smaller one C to the area of the larger one B will be the area of the larger one B to the sum that is A. You can construct fascinating spirals from these series of pentagons inside of pentagons, and why not? For the architects understood the power of that verse from Scripture, that God created the world "by measure and number and weight" (Wisd. 11:20), or, as the poet Blake would say:

> To see a World in a Grain of Sand,
> And a Heaven in a Wild Flower,
> Hold Infinity in the palm of your hand
> And Eternity in an hour.
> ("Auguries of Innocence," 1–4)

Or think of Dante's *Divine Comedy*, dedicated to the Holy Trinity and to Christ, the incarnate Word of God. Dante knew he would divide the work into the three realms of the hereafter, Hell, Purgatory, and Heaven. Or rather he saw that God had already created the moral universe in such a way, reflecting His triune Being. What kind of meter, then, would be fittest for Dante's poem? He invented terza rima for it, a system of interlocking tercets, whose first and third lines would rhyme, while the second line would rhyme with the first and third lines of the next tercet. I could go on for a long time describing the artistry with which Dante makes each realm resemble or echo or foreshadow or fulfill the others, so that you do not really understand the *Inferno* until you have finished your journey through the *Purgatorio* and the *Paradiso*. This is not the case, as in the modern novel, because strands of the plot have yet to play out to their end. It is rather as if you were to be presented with a vast canvas with its various persons and stories simultaneously displayed, and not just as happening to occur at a single moment though separate from one another, but as intimately interrelated, from a point of view that comprehends the whole. In this way, a work of art like *The Divine Comedy* or like a medieval cathedral was meant to reflect, though in man's piecemeal and temporal way, the all-enfolding, all-circumscribing eternal vision of God, and of His creation as present to Him in what Eliot calls "the still point of the turning world," where the dance is (*Four Quartets*, "Burnt Norton").

The Beauty of the Particular

And yet beauty cannot be reduced to abstract laws. These may be beautiful, but they are far from exhausting what beauty is. They mainly help to point our way. Let me not suggest that the five-petaled flower is beautiful because it is a biological manifestation of the Fibonacci sequence of numbers, but rather that the Fibonacci sequence somehow reflects the beauty we find in the five-petaled flower. For beauty resists all reduction, all programming.

To see why, we may turn to what I have often called the most beautiful object of contemplation in all of the physical world. Let the blind poet Milton tell us what he misses the most, now that his eyes no longer see:

Thus with the year
Seasons return, but not to me returns
Day, or the sweet approach of even or morn,
Or sight of vernal bloom, or summer's rose,
Or flocks, or herds, or human face divine.
(*Paradise Lost*, 3.40–44)

The "human face divine": notice how Milton has bracketed the face with the two adjectives, human and divine, with the stress laid on the second, because the human face *is divine*, as man is made in the image of God. We do not mean that man looks like God, as Hercules might resemble his father, Zeus, but that man is intelligent, possesses a spiritual being, is oriented toward the knowledge of all that is, and is meant not only to know but to love with a love that can soar beyond natural affection. The dog is faithful, and indeed is man's best friend, but for all his fine goodness and loyalty, the dog cannot say, "I give myself to you forever, come what may," because the dog has no notion of the passage of time and cannot reach beyond the present, either forward with anticipation and promise, or backward with deliberate recollection and consideration. When we look at a human face, if the full humanity is present, as with an old man creased with a life of kindness and wisdom, or love and sadness, we are beholding a mystery. It is as if we had come to the threshold of a vast world, a universe of meaning, not closed in on itself but always open to the infinite, and all the more beautiful because it is destined, in this life, to pass into oblivion.

And I find that Darwin cannot show us how to take that infinite leap from the subhuman to the human: from the shrewd ape to the being capable of saying, with the psalmist:

When I look at thy heavens, the work of thy fingers, the
moon and the stars which thou hast established; what is

man that thou art mindful of him, and the son of man
that thou dost care for him? Yet thou hast made him little
less than God, and dost crown him with glory and honor.
(Ps. 8:3–5)

Reductions falsify. The human person is by nature oriented toward
the infinite, and there are no gradations between grasping a finite
thing and apprehending the mystery and the beauty of the infinite
God. It is not true that you can go from a lot of repetitions of a
thing to a grasp of endlessness itself, just by taking baby steps. I
suspect rather that already in the small human child, the possibility
of transcending discrete events or discrete impressions of a finite
object is present and active, though latent and without words to
define itself; the child will gaze up at the endless sky for the sheer
wonder of it. Whatever may be the origin of the human body, this
orientation is irreducible. It is like the difference between the ink on
a page and the ideas the spots of ink convey. The ideas themselves
may be expressed in words but are irreducible to them — as many a
mathematician knows, when he sees a truth before he has the words
or even the numbers to express what he sees.

Let me go further. I have read the first-person account of a
disgruntled explorer, that the natives he met in the Congo were no
more intelligent than apes. He based his judgment on the fact that
no matter how much trouble he took to show them how the steam
engines he used worked, they could not grasp how to repair them,
so that as soon as they broke down a little, they might as well have
been buried forever under the jungle vegetation. I am not persuaded.
I recall a scene from the film *How Green Was My Valley*, in which
the parson is trying to instruct young Huw Morgan in mathematical ratios, and he asks the boy a question about water flowing out
of a bathtub from two holes of different sizes. "Drilling holes in a

bathtub!" laughs the good Mrs. Morgan, who cannot make the leap, or is too impatient to make it, or sees no immediate practicality in making it, from the function of bathtubs to the power of numbers. But what if you took, at birth, a baby born to an Aboriginal tribe of Australia, one of those tribes whose language did not name a number past four or five, and raised him up in a world of mathematics. I am not saying that the *environment* would make him but that what he already was by virtue of his human nature would find ready avenues of development. Man, wherever he is, wherever he is born, is that creature that is, in his form, *capax universi*: capable of apprehending (not necessarily comprehending) every existent.

There is a second thing about human beauty that cannot be captured by reduction, and this is something that Donatello understood better than did the ancient Greek sculptors whose work he sometimes, quite literally, dug out of the rubble and earth about Rome. The beauty of the face is ineradicable from the kind of being the human creature is, and also from the *particularities* of its features, the stamp upon it of what the person has seen and done and lived and loved and *thought*. Thus do we find perfect symmetry, a sort of robotic predictability and elementary perfection, an offense in the human face; for the face is the outward manifestation of the unique person. The beauty mark is both a mark — that is, a blemish — and a thing of beauty, because of its distinctness, its uniqueness; so also the charm of a crooked smile, or the habitual tilt of the head, or the cowlick that cannot be pasted to lie flat on a billiard ball, much less on the hilly contours of the human head; so the relationship between the strong eye and the weaker eye, which though they blink in unison, do not quite look identical. And that is why Donatello's sculpture of the prophet Habakkuk, a bald and ugly man with much patient suffering stamped upon his features, affects us far more profoundly than does many a "perfect" curly-headed and youthful Greek god, who never suffered and never would, and who somehow never attains the mark of individuality. Donatello's fellow citizens of Florence seem to have grasped the point, and so they nicknamed his sculpture *Lo Zuccone*—"Baldy," or, more literally, the "Big Pumpkin Head." They felt the power of it, and they knew that only the greatest of sculptors could have delivered it.

I have sometimes asked my students to consider, with the psalmist, "thy heavens, the work of thy fingers" (8:3) and to imagine that God had made the stars indistinguishable from one another, all the same color, a blank white, all the same magnitude, and all set apart from those nearest by exactly the same distance, as in a gridwork. The very thought of it is appalling. Would we gaze upon it in wonder? We would turn from it in disgust or in boredom. The beauty even of a hill or a tree is, in part, that it is *this hill, this tree*: the hill, for example, that I climbed all the time when I was a boy, in the woods a half mile behind my house. It was a tumbled-up heap of boulders and soil, left by the retreating glaciers when the last Ice Age was over, where nothing could grow but scrub birches, blueberries, wild roses, and other vegetation hugging the ground. The boulders had gotten covered over with a layer of wind-blown dust over the ages, and these formed them into a hill, but often you would find a crevice, like a crack in the earth under your feet, and you could never tell how far down the crack went. From that hill I could see my town below, with its mostly unplotted streets straggling up the side of the mountain that faced me across the valley, and the tallest building of all, the church, with its cupola and cross extended toward the sky, but from my vantage a thing of mystery far below. I was lonely in that town when I was not with my family and my many cousins, but I did love it, even though—or perhaps also because—it was also pocked and pitted, and enormous mounds of coal flakes, called culm, dominated the scene, and they were either bare and gleaming with a dull blue-black, or they, too, had gotten swept by dust and soil, and small birches grew up along their sides here and there. I loved it because it was a human place, though also a place still mysterious to man, with small and ordinary and beautiful things in plain sight, such as the apple trees here and there growing wild.

Now, I might say that beauty is akin to truth in at least these two of its fundamental features, and in its existential power for any intellectual being. First, we find beauty in the kind of thing that exists, that which presents us, as glowing with the light of intelligibility, the general or the universal; so when we see that there is such a thing as a deer, not this one or that one but the form they share, that unites them, that makes them intelligible to us, it is like coming upon a theorem of great reach and power, or like gazing, with the mind, into the intricacies of carbon atoms, and seeing in them the possibilities of stars and planets, and this life of ours on earth. Second, we find beauty in the particular thing that exists, this deer and not that one, or this kind of creature and not that kind; this hill that is like countless others but that is always and tenaciously itself and no other; and we mark the distinctions, just as we mark the homely lights and shadows in a face we have grown to know and love. And as no other physical creature we know of is oriented toward all truth, so no other physical creature is struck by beauty, and for the same spiritual reason: we desire to know; we desire to love. A dog sees; but a dog does not behold. A dog knows things that are so; but he does not long to know the truth.

The Cult of Ugliness

Let us suppose now that we deny the objective existence of the beautiful. Let us focus then on the two properties I have described: the first, the power of the small feature to reflect the greater or the whole, which power we may also view as the whole making itself present in each smallest part; the second, the individuating, that which, to cite the poet Gerard Manley Hopkins,

> Deals out that being indoors each one dwells,
> Selves, goes itself: Myself, it speaks and spells,
> Crying, What I do is me: for that I came.
> ("As Kingfishers Catch Fire," 5–8)

What is the artist, the poet, or the architect to do? Imagine now a vast bare stretch of wall, unbroken by any features. That is a parody of the self-similar: we know that the great will be no different from the small, because there is no difference from one patch of wall to the next. It possesses the bleakness but not the stark beauty of a desert. For there is a shimmering in the undulating sands, and we can see the riffles of the wind that have marked the dunes as waves rendered in what seems neither solid nor liquid but somehow both at once. But the long bare wall is not like that. It possesses the uniformity but not the color and the vastness and the wonder of the blue sky above, which is not really uniform either but shades in blue from the horizon to wherever the sun is shining, and we see the sun itself not as a great bare light bulb but as a burning presence that, when we squint, shoots out rays of glory.

No one finds the bare wall beautiful. We may find the blocks of color in a painting by Mondrian to be moderately interesting, but it was quite revealing, in a disappointing way, when the curators of a British museum learned accidentally that they had hung one of his paintings upside down for seventy years, and no one could tell the difference. Mondrian does not offend; but neither does he attract, inspire, stir the soul to wonder. What does offend is the bareness or barrenness that is meant to reduce the human observer to insignificance. It is the reverse of Blake's wonder-struck lines about the grain of sand and the wildflower, that exalt us and humble us at once. We are to be *intimidated* by vastness and inhumanity. Think of the tremendous glass and steel structures that rise like robotic monsters from our cities. The flash and glance of light upon them may sometimes please the eye for a short time. But no one finds them beautiful. They are oppressive. They are towers of Babel that assume that men are ants; and perhaps the ambition and the humiliation — *not humbling, but humiliation* — are the same phenomenon viewed from two different perspectives. The capital of a pillar in a Gothic cathedral bears the traces of careful human hands, and their often boisterous expressiveness; so does the very craftsmanship raise up the soul of the man who carved the figures, taking him up into the whole vast vision, which finds a place for every individual person; but each panel of glass in the tower is indistinguishable from the next, and the human hand might as well have been the extended arm of a machine, without love, without vision, without feeling, without thought; and though the towers claw the sky, the men they harbor have no real home there, unless they manage somehow to piece out a little bit of life within.

Then there is the ugliness of chaos. Again, this is not the orderly disorder or the homely particularity of a real human neighborhood but a refusal to recognize order at all. Artists have been encouraged to despise mere "representationalism," and the result has been a calamitous loss of countless techniques, the knowledge of the hands passed down through the generations, so that we rightly wonder whether we can have another Norman Rockwell, painting all kinds of human beings in their attitudes and gestures and expressions and actions, let alone another Titian or Rembrandt. We can laugh at artists tossing balloons of color onto a blank canvas, or producing works that might as well have been splashed by apes or sprinkler systems with kinks in them. But the chaos is not always so obvious. We have it in its form as slovenliness, revealing a kind of spiritual and intellectual deficit; think of the old buildings with all their fine work in wooden or plaster moldings, in finials, tapered columns, eaves, baseboards, and wainscot, "renovated" by removal, or marred by the pasting on of a cheapjack door or gate or entryway that makes the thing look like a sculpture by Michelangelo, painted in garish colors by a not-very-talented ten-year-old. The slovenliness, or listlessness, borders on incoherence too; think of city streets, themselves as it were whole works of human art that grew up with a kind of organic naturalness, houses and buildings echoing one another but each distinct; and see them now with buildings torn down, some here, some there, scattershot, and replaced by things that look like great plastic boxes, with blazing signs. Why are our eyes not constantly sore? We have gotten accustomed to it.

And now this cult of ugliness has infected what we think about our own selves. One lie leads to another, and so we continue to disentangle them here. The next lie is this: *there is no such thing as human nature.*

THE FOURTH LIE

Human Nature Does Not Exist

WHAT STANDS AGAINST the plans of those who would remake the world according to their own imaginations, which inevitably means according to their own dreams of power and glory for themselves and those like them? It is not so much the stubbornness of earth and water, of rocks and trees, of a world of plants and animals that resists our proud attempts to squeeze it into molds. Thank God for those! But the first and most intractable object of resistance is in man himself, in his nature. That is why all utopian dreamers and utopian pests that ravage the poor peace in this world must deny that there is such a thing as human nature, instead supposing that we can squeeze man into the right mold by the power of education, which means, in reality, by the force of dogged attempts to indoctrinate and to compel him to behave in ways that are counter to his nature, and administering correctives, whether pharmacological, economic, military, or judicial, when the pressure of falsehood proves too great for certain souls to endure and they rebel.

But first, let us address the fact of the matter. There is such a thing as human nature.

Universal Languages

The evidence is overwhelming, but it is strangely easy to overlook, not because it is hard to find but because it is so near to us, and it so pervades every feature of our lives that we take it for granted and do not even notice it anymore.

Suppose you go to a land that for you is strange and faraway—Mongolia, for example. You see dogs in the street. You will recognize them immediately as dogs, though many of them will be mongrels, and some of the breeds may strike you as unusual. Still, if you have any experience of dogs, you will "read" them right. You see the tail wagging merrily—or it is tucked under, waving just a bit, because the dog is not sure of you. You see the ears perked up—or flattened back. You hear the kind of bark the dog gives—sharp and bright, or a low growl, or an insistent series of bellows, or a howl, or a yipe with the note of a puppy in it—and you guess, correctly, what the dog is trying to "say" to you. You have no idea what the dog's name is, if he has a name at all, and you don't know what the words for "come here" are in Mongolian, but you crouch down to make yourself small, you slap your knee, you open your hand, palm forward, and you speak in a gentle and inviting way, and the dog comes over to you, sniffing, because that's his main way of figuring out whether you are good or bad.

Needless to say, the dog hasn't gone to dog school, hasn't been burdened with canine propaganda, hasn't been "socialized" into his behavior; it is all the natural behavior of dogs. Yet it certainly is social, because the dog is by nature a social animal, and it certainly does show forth a basic friendliness toward man, whom the dog accepts as a member of his pack, or as the leaders of his pack. This is not controversial.

Now you meet a pack of little boys, playing. Again, you do not know the tongue. You have a vague idea of the kind of food they eat, and when they take their meals. You have another vague idea of the kinds of work the people are mainly occupied with. But the only way you can really approach those boys is by taking for granted innumerable features of human nature.

You smile, and not with the frozen gleam of a confidence man. You probably do quite a number of things with your body that you are not aware of—the way you tilt your head, or nod, or approach in an easygoing manner; the tone of your voice as you try to utter a word of approval or welcome that you hope they will understand; you will be speaking a language that is universal to mankind. Perhaps they are playing a game with a ball and something to hit it with, or perhaps they are trying to hit each other with the ball. Your mind begins to guess at the rules, because you are sure there are rules, because you know what boys are like: they are inveterate and restless inventors of games.

One of the boys evidently breaks the rules, whatever they are, because you see them stop and start pointing and gesturing and arguing back and forth, and you know that boys dislike a cheat and despise a spoilsport. Were you in ancient Rome, you might hear them chant what the poet Horace records for us: "If you do right in everything, / You'll grow up to be the king!" (*Epistles*, 1.1.59– 60). Then one of the boys, apparently the one who was accused, ducks his head a bit sheepishly and kicks the dirt, and the game resumes—because if you do try to get away with a foul, the right thing to do is to admit it when you're called for it. This, too, you understand, while you still have only a vague idea of what the boys are doing. All this, too, is a part of the universal human language, even the shrug, the hangdog look, the dirt-kicking. It is arbitrary, perhaps, in the sense that we can imagine another kind of creature on another planet doing different things to convey the same attitudes and intentions, but it is not arbitrary at all in this world of ours. It comes as naturally as learning to walk.

You see a mother with an infant child. She is gazing into the child's eyes and making funny faces to cause the child to smile and laugh. It is exactly the same as if she were an Aboriginal in the outback desert of Australia. She might as well be a Guarani on the banks of the Amazon. She might be an Inuit woman living in the wastes of the Mackenzie Delta. Giotto paints Mary looking into the eyes of the Christ Child with an intensity that every mother can understand. It is the overwhelming maternal force. The child, who has never read a book about nature or nurture, does what every healthy child and, as far as I can gather, even every sickly child will do. He gazes back at his mother. He is doing more than learning. He is communicating. If you toss a baby into the water, I am told, he will immediately begin to move his arms and legs to swim, just as he moved about in the liquid-filled womb. We do not do that to him — we dare not risk his life. But we toss babies into water all the time, into the sea of human communication and meaning, and they soak in it, paddle happily in it, take it into themselves, play with it, *in ways that no dog can.* In this sense, there are no human infants but only human beings who have not yet learned to do certain coordinated things with their tongues, lips, teeth, breath, and vocal cords; from the beginning, the human being is *homo loquens,* "man the speaker."

Social Man

Man, we sometimes hear, has certain physical needs that he cannot easily fulfill alone, so that he enters into society strictly for his self-preservation, but if we could fulfill the needs without the society, we might do so and be none the worse for it. This line of thinking underlies every theory of the so-called social contract. It presumes a purely "natural man," pre-social, a being of whose existence we have not the slightest evidence, and thus it attributes to human societies those features that the arbitrary circumstances of human existence recommended to men as fit for their survival. When the circumstances change, the societies change with them.

As always, we must take care to disentangle strands of truth from the fundamental error. Men who live near the sea will have ways of life fit for the place, its opportunities, its dangers; and those ways of life will not be the same as the ways that men on the steppes of Eurasia will find amenable. Technological development will not proceed uniformly. What foundry skills are even conceivable when you live in a region of permafrost, or in the lushly overgrown jungles of the Congo or the Amazon? You will not find iron plowshares wherever you find human beings, because you will not always find iron, or land that can be plowed.

But look at the things you will always find. You will always find language, which is social in its essence, and it will always be more than a set of primitive and unalterable signals, such as birds of a feather give to one another. Indeed, we know of no truly primitive language, in the sense of a language with a tiny vocabulary and only a few ways of distinguishing one idea from another. If languages "evolve," they do so by changing the vocabulary to fit the needs of the time, and, if anything, by streamlining the grammar, making it *less complex*: the grammar of modern English, compared to the grammar of Old English, which was already well along the way toward simplification, is as a hydraulic lift compared with an interlocking system of gears and pulleys. Gone are the seven or eight cases of nouns and adjectives in our parent language, Indo-European; gone are almost all of the personal endings on our verbs; gone is the grammatically signaled distinction between actions performed once and those performed habitually; most of the old "strong" verbs that formed their past tense by the change of the interior vowel have been assimilated to the "weak" form, characterized by the dental suffixes -*ed* and -*t*, so that we say *climbed* instead of *clomb*, and *helped* instead of *holp*. You want complexity? Take a look at the fifteen or sixteen verbal forms in Guarani — forms that signal whether you're certain of something that happened a long time ago, or you were uncertain of a thing but now you're sure, or something is going to happen soon, or something is going on currently but perhaps not right here and now, and so on. Or look at the verbal system of ancient Hebrew. My college students, poorly instructed in the easy contours of English grammar, have a hard time distinguishing the passive and the active voice. They should be thankful we have no middle voice, as developed in early modern Swedish, and as was alive and well in ancient Greek. They should be even more thankful that we do not have the seven voices or aspects of the ancient Hebrew verb: active, passive, causative active, causative passive, intensive active, intensive passive, and reflexive. No, as soon as you have man, you have a linguistic universe.

And a social universe too. One of the fundamental errors of social contract theories is, as I have already discussed, their utilitarianism, which they derive from their own parent, the materialism of Epicurus, as described in immortal poetry by his most cogent follower, the Roman poet Lucretius. Men enter into society *in order to get something good out of it*, or, more urgently, *to avoid something bad*. True enough it is that by themselves men do starve or live a life hardly to be called human at all. But men never have lived by themselves. It is not just need that impels them. They are oriented to it by their nature. Men are the creatures with a fullness of personhood shining in the face: they are meant to look at one another, in friendship. Their need for one another is also a delight in one another; they are made by Love, for love, and, as the poet Wordsworth says, "we have all of us one human heart."

The sense that man is for man, not by economic necessity but by nature, is also universal to human cultures. "I am a man," says one of the characters in Terence's comedy *The Self-Tormentor*, "and so nothing human can be alien to me" (1.1.77). "Every man's death diminishes me," says the poet and Christian divine, John Donne, "because I am involved in mankind" (*Devotions upon Emergent Occasions*, "Meditation 17"). Donne means the participle "involved" quite literally: *wrapped up in, enveloped by, inextricable from* mankind. Rousseau said that man, born free, became enslaved by society, and therefore he would have his ideal child Emile brought up apart from human intercourse until his fifteenth year. Thus do madness, cruelty, and sentimentality dance hand in hand, the Three Ingratitudes, foisting and burdening rather than giving, snatching rather than receiving. We are more social than the social dog, not less, because the strands of relationship into which we are born extend far beyond the bounds of our personal life on earth. The great-grandfather I never knew, who, as I have heard, was tagged with the nickname *Isolano*, "Man on an Island," because he was a loner, and who seems to have imparted to my father's father a trace of his surliness, is more real to me than the dog's own mother is to the dog once he no longer nurses at her teats. I hope that my great-grandchildren to come will read these words I write, and will say, with some pride, that the blood in my veins flows yet in their own. Our need for one another is not utilitarian. Cicero was no traditionalist when it came to trusting the old stories of the gods, and so we might think he would be friendly to the Epicurean philosophy that did away with any notion that the gods had to do with us at all. And his dearest friend, Atticus, was an Epicurean. But when the Epicureans base friendship upon utility, Cicero replies that though friendship does provide us with many things of use, that is not its origin at all, and in fact, the origin of friendship is "more ancient and more beautiful," as it comes from love itself, so that we should guard against people who "cultivate the appearance of friendship" because they aim to gain by it (*On Friendship*, 8.26). Such would be the bond uniting a pack of thieves that find one another, in current circumstances, mutually beneficial; and as soon as the circumstances turn, so do the coats of the thieves.

Again, there is no such thing, and there never has been such a thing, as "natural" man without society, for man is a social being to the core, and the societies he forms are more or less in concord with both his biological and his intellectual nature; nor are his biology and his intellect separate things. Think of it. From the moment of conception, all the latent powers of man are unfolding, so long as no internal flaw or external influence obstructs them; the child in the womb already experiences things not as a fish or a dog does, but, incipiently, as a social and intellectual being; so does the child stare deeply into his mother's eyes, and wave his hands at the motion of the mobile above his crib, stirred by a gentle breeze. And these features of his being, these faculties of his soul, are bound to one another also, because the greatest of all the delights of friendship is to share with a kindred spirit the fruits of your investigation, your inventiveness, your thought, your contemplation, your prayer.

Experiments upon and against Human Nature

If you take human nature not merely as a given but as a gift to be cherished, even human nature fallen and marred by sin, you may be like an architect who sees in the material he works with — hemlock planks, cedar shingles, clay tiles, granite, marble to shave and dress — both an inherent beauty and the means to express what he can best express in them and through them. Master carpenters understand the principle. Why would birch make a fine wood for these intricately patterned posts? Why use rosewood for the sounding board of a guitar? You work with the grain; you work with nature, and nature gives you the very means to transcend what she gives you, which still is in accord with nature.

Thus, too, there need be no division between man's art and the nature he works with. Here I turn to Shakespeare's *The Winter's Tale*, a play that examines both human nature and the arts that are natural to us. When the shepherd lass Perdita—a foundling, actually a princess, though she does not know it, while her natural nobility shines forth from her humble dress and circumstances unbidden—says to King Polixenes that she won't keep streaked flowers in her garden, because she has heard it said that "there is an art, which in their piedness shares / With great creating Nature," he replies, gently and intelligently,

> Say there be;
> Yet Nature is made better by no mean
> But Nature makes that mean; so over that art
> Which you say adds to Nature, is an art
> That Nature makes.
> (4.4.87–91)

She is not persuaded, though the play she and King Polixenes dwell in is about, among other things, the inter-involvement, in human action and in the plan and design of Providence, of human will and the grace of God; of art, whether human or divine, and the nature that gives rise to the art, and that the art honors and ennobles. Perdita is artless, in the sense that she has no soul for guile, and therefore, Shakespeare suggests, is she filled with a kind of natural art, as her lover the prince Florizel says:

> What you do
> Still betters what is done. When you speak, sweet,
> I'd have you do it ever; when you sing,
> I'd have you buy and sell so; so give alms,
> Pray so; and for the ordering your affairs,

To sing them too. When you do dance, I wish you
A wave of the sea, that you might ever do
Nothing but that—move still, still so,
And own no other function. Each your doing,
So singular in each particular,
Crowns what you are doing in the present deeds,
That all your acts are queens.
(4.4.135–146)

The praise is potent indeed: in Perdita, a young girl of consummate virtue, art springs from nature and nature enhances and merges with art, so that, as we look upon her with the wonder she deservedly merits, we move deeper into both moral and human reality. I will add, too, that you cannot reverse the sexes here without absurdity: no woman ever says such things about a man, because it is in the nature of the man to see the woman as the finest and most natural work of art. So Adam once looked with wonder upon the new and innocent Eve.

Before the Industrial Revolution, man was not wealthy enough, nor were his rulers and masters powerful enough, to attempt social experiments *against* reality, some of which, ironically, were prompted by his increasing unease with the drab and ugly and soul-smothering industrial world he had created. As in a large family, some of whose cousins are handsome because they have inherited the family looks, and some of whose cousins are ugly for the same reason, but all are cousins nonetheless, so, too, with modern social movements based on these premises: either that man is infinitely malleable, like a sort of ideal plastic, so that you can pour him into whatever mold you will, or that man has been deformed by society, so that if you scrub away its scurf you may come to the genuine article lying underneath. Those amiable poets Robert Southey and Samuel Taylor Coleridge planned to settle in the woods of Pennsylvania, despite the handicap of their knowing nothing about farming, lumbering, hunting, trapping, and fishing, to set up an ideal communal life that they called "Pantisocracy." Fortunately for social and literary history, it came to nothing. At Oneida, in upstate New York, onetime Congregationalist minister John Humphrey Noyes established a community devoted to "complex marriage," which in actual practice meant no marriage at all, as everyone was encouraged to bed down with everyone else (men with women, that is), so long as the woman gave her consent. Records were kept, lest human nature intrude and some man fall in love with a woman and want her for himself alone, so that if John were paying too much attention to Mary, they would be kept apart by the tyrant-god of their experimental lives. One of the women in the community recalled a ceremony in which little girls who had grown too attached to their wax dolls — for at Oneida, such a sense of ownership, of devoted and exclusive love, must be obliterated — were made to step up to an open stove and cast them into the mouth of that little hell.

Jean-Jacques Rousseau cried out that man was born free but is everywhere in chains. His disciple and heir, Karl Marx, as pure a utopian schemer as ever walked the earth — pure, that is, in his all-consuming hatred of man — went on, like a new kind of Baptist wearing a hair shirt on his soul, to establish the grounds of a society conceived as against all of man's natural devotions, to kin, to the place of his birth, to his nation, and to God. The result was some hundreds of millions of people butchered, and many a thriving human culture despoiled, corrupted, or obliterated.

The experiments continue because they *can*. No farmer of old would consent for a minute to have his son put on a girl's dress and prance about with affected femininity. No such son could even imagine it. The fields need plowing. The big animals need tending.

The boy's mother herself would be encouraging him in his developing manhood, because good harvests make the difference between plenty and penury, or sometimes between survival and starvation. But now? Our wealth protects us from the immediate physical and economic consequences of our stupidity, just as modern building materials permit architects to construct ceilings that look as if they are going to collapse on our heads, or towers with a bend in them that look as if they must topple like Babel; the experiments go on.

The experiments do not succeed. The Israelis attempted to integrate female with male soldiers, partly because they had accepted the utopian dream of sexual indistinguishability and collective families, but partly because they were a small nation surrounded by enemies, and they needed all the bodies they could find who were able to tote a rifle. But they learned quickly that the experiment did not work. Morale cratered. Men were men and women were women. The men naturally hung back to protect the women; and that meant, too, that the men competed against one another for the attention of the women; and the women, for their part, were always the weakest chain-link in any operation that required physical prowess. So the Israelis separated the sexes again, because they valued survival more than ideology. Meanwhile, my own United States senator has expressed her disappointment that Congress failed to enact a law to expose women to the draft, and a military draft, be it noted, is solely for massive numbers—numbers to fill the ranks of the infantry, grunt soldiers on the ground; not medics, not quartermasters, not camp trainers, but the army's foot, those who suffer the highest casualties but those without whom not one square mile of enemy territory can be seized and held.

Experiments against reality—who engages in them, if not those who hate the reality they experiment against? Thus is every utopian a secret or not-so-secret hater of man. Let us take the modern school as a utopian project. At first glance it may seem to betray all that

Rousseau had in mind when he kept his imaginary Emile out of human intercourse until his fifteenth year. If anything, the modern school is like an all-pervading fungus that takes up more and more years, and more and more time during the day, all in the blessed name of education, and in the not-so-blessed name of "socialization," when, to judge by the results, precious little education goes on there that would not naturally come to young people just from being around decent things to read, and such socialization as does occur produces young people who are peevish, sullen, suspicious, ungrateful, vain of their small accomplishments, and eager to form cliques for the heady delight of making outsiders miserable. Surely Rousseau did not want any of that—though, in his treatment of his own children, the man was a monster.

Yet the school shares with Rousseau the same denaturing of the young person, the same refusal to see that a child belongs in a network of natural human relationships, those that involve a piety that works in two directions, from the parent to the child and from the child to the parent, and under *parent* we include also those who exercise, in some fashion or to some degree, fatherly or motherly authority, such as priests, ministers, uncles and aunts, elder brothers and sisters, civic leaders, police, adult neighbors, and so forth. Charles Dickens, in his ferocious satire against the utilitarian education of his day, *Hard Times*, well understood that the schoolmaster Gradgrind's error lay not only in his contempt for the human imagination, as his instructors were to impart only "facts, facts, facts" to the children, planting only those and rooting out everything else. It is that he likewise—and, I say, inevitably—sinned against the whole human child his school was to teach, in severing them from that same piety. The heroine of the story, Sissy Jupe, has been enrolled in his school because of her own father's right and proper sense of duty; he wanted to give her a good education, away from the sometimes-raffish circuses he worked in, but he mistook where that education was to be found. Sissy, irremovably loyal to her father (whom we never meet; he dies, far from his daughter), is taken in to Gradgrind's household, where she moderates to some degree the unhappiness of his own daughter Louisa and his son Tom. It is only her determined ministration that saves Louisa from ruin at the hands of an unscrupulous man about town, and the energetic and artful dodging managed by her friends in the circus that gets Tom safely out of England before the arm of the law seizes him for grand theft.

John Dewey, that Maoist sympathizer who is largely responsible for the structure and the condition of modern American schools, wanted to produce—I use the word advisedly, because his thought was dully mechanistic, and though he himself retained a wistful liking for such things as poetry, his system could really find little place for them—democratic citizens, and he failed to see, as so many utopians have failed before him, that the citizen is born from the faithful son and daughter in a family, the devoted parishioner in a church, the helpful and reliable neighbor on a farm road or a city block. If you want real citizens, rather than functionaries; if you want to raise sons and daughters for a nation, not counters in an electoral game; if you want people who raise the moral tenor of your land, and who beautify it by their works and words and very persons; you cannot do so by pretending that they are but indefinitely ductile and malleable lumps of rationality and desire. The family, as Pope Leo XIII affirmed in all his social encyclicals, is the seedbed of anything that can genuinely be called a "society."

After the Fall

Jonathan Swift had little patience for people experimenting upon human nature. In his fantastical and many-faceted satire, *Gulliver's Travels*, Swift inveighs against both the folly of man and all quasi-mechanical attempts to cure the folly. In his last voyage, the one that seems, according to many critics, to drive him quite mad, Gulliver finds himself in the land of the Houyhnhnms, rational horses, who think, and talk, and use their hooves deftly for handiwork, and live entirely reasonable lives, so much so that they cannot understand Gulliver when he tries to describe what life elsewhere in the world is like. They have no word for "lying," so they suppose he has said "the thing that was not." Meanwhile, they must overcome their natural disgust for Gulliver, because in his looks and his form he resembles the detestable creatures they live among, the Yahoos, who embody all the vices of Swift's European and English contemporaries, without the veneer of rationality. The Yahoos combine idiocy, vanity, squalor, treachery, and uselessness to themselves and to other Yahoos, so that the Houyhnhnms can make very little of them — far less than Europeans have made of their biological kinsman, the horse.

Gulliver lives long enough with the Houyhnhnms so that when he finally returns home to England, he can hardly stand being in the same room with his wife and his children without feeling the need to retch. And the critics I have in mind, with whom I disagree somewhat and with hesitation, say that Gulliver is wrong to feel this way, and that Swift has directed his satire against the Houyhnhnms themselves, and not only or not even primarily against the Yahoos. I don't know; "horse sense," as you might call it, is not the same as Enlightenment rationalism, and the Houyhnhnms do not resemble the various hyper-rational and yet cruel rulers of Laputa, whose heads are so far in the clouds they must have servants nearby to smack them in the ears with beanbags to get their attention to a statement or a question, and to smack them in the mouths with the same to get them to speak; and this, too, while the servants are making free with the Laputans' wives.

Yet the point is well taken, and I can agree so far: we must live in this world as it is, with man as he is, whom Shakespeare's Hamlet well describes neither as a Yahoo nor as a Houyhnhnm, but as something far more than the latter, and far other than the former:

> What a piece of work is a man, How noble in reason, how infinite in faculty, In form and moving how express and admirable, In action how like an Angel, In apprehension how like a god, The beauty of the world, The paragon of animals. And yet to me, what is this quintessence of dust? Man delights not me. (*Hamlet*, 2.2.311–316)

The psalmist says that man is "little less than God" (Ps. 8:5), and the sacred author of Genesis tells us that God, after the great flood, looked upon man and said that "the imagination of man's heart is evil from his youth" (Gen. 8:21). "The greatness and the wretchedness of man are so plain to see," says Pascal, "that the true religion must needs teach us that there is some great principle of greatness in man, and a great principle of wretchedness too" (*Pensees*, fragment 430; translation mine). Nor can education efface the contradiction, for "all your enlightenment can only bring you to realize that you can find neither good nor truth within yourselves." And why not? Pascal continues, criticizing the philosophers, whom we may say take the place here of all rationalists, all the schemers either of social perfection or personal elevation beyond the ordinary run of men: "Your main maladies are the pride that takes you away from God and the concupiscence that binds you to the earth; and they," the rationalists, "have done nothing but entertain at least one of these maladies."

To live in the world as it is, and not as we would have it be, is to take man as he is, acknowledging the fallenness of his nature, his propensity to wickedness, but also the possibility—I add, by grace alone—that he may look upon the God in whose image he has been made. In some fashion or other, every utopian project, every deeply antisocial attempt to fashion a human society apart from or against human nature as it is, denies either that man is made in God's image, or that man has fallen, or both. The results, at the extremes, are a grim police state in which, in the name of the great social leap forward that is to come, everyone is a potential threat to everyone else, and everyone is reduced to an atom of the collective will, or a garish sybaritic "freedom" that enslaves people to their desires, captures them in the tangles of a welfare state, and in the name of society reduces men to atoms of individual will, and again, every man's hand is against everyone else. In both the old drab Soviet Union and the gaudy new and improved United States, the problem of the human heart is simply evaded or ignored: having the "correct" political positions supplies the need, and schooling is thus devoted to producing clever idiots, or worse, clever beasts, or worst of all, devils.

When I was a boy, the residuum of the old ways still clung to our lives, and so we were trooped, once a month, all four hundred of us children, to the church across the street for Confession. That was to work with human nature: fallen human nature. The nuns were too canny to believe that children were naturally good, and thus that they could follow wherever their desires might lead. For often I desire what is wrong, and it may be many years before I even see that it was wrong, if I ever do see it at all. People may carp at the supposed iron severity of the nuns who taught us. As I look back on it, I see that most of them were nice people, and that their occasional outbursts of temper came less from natural wickedness and spite than from overwork, the ingratitude of parishioners, and the turmoil within their order—for that was no calm time to be in religious garb. Yet though my hair was pulled once and though

Sr. Eugene in aggressive overconfidence promised my eighth grade class that she would give them an entire month free of homework for every scholarship to a local Catholic high school I won—there were three I applied to, and to her dismay I swept the table—most of us arrived at school by foot, there was no security guard, we had a full hour for lunch and could leave the grounds at will, the classes with up to fifty students in a room almost always went on without disruption, and thus did we small sinners, treated as sinners, enjoy far more freedom than do students in schools now.

Thus do we uncover a strange paradox. If you understand that man is fallen, you will do all you can to inculcate in children and in young people, whose passions are apt to get ahead of their reason, a strong sense of what is right and wrong, and the strength of will to resist temptations. Inner restraints lighten the need for outer restraints. Similarly, social restraints lighten the need for legal restraints. That permits plenty of freedom of action, a pragmatic freedom, daily enjoyed in ways great and small. But if you indulge the fantasy that man is not fallen, and you do not train up the reason-directed will to overmaster the passion-directed will, the chaos of your streets will soon resemble the chaos of your souls, or else you submit to what is effectively a police state. At the extremes, you will either have San Francisco as the city is now, where a careless and hard-hearted leniency pretends to be mercy, and the homeless multiply in numbers and in real misery, and people's front yards stink of trash and feces, or you will retreat behind the bars and walls of a "gated community." Short of those extremes, you will have American towns and cities characterized by disorder or by a false, reduced order, the orderliness of a blank canvas, streets mostly empty, and no children swarming over the neighborhood.

Let us come to cases. When I was in high school, the sense that sexual intercourse before marriage was wrong was still pretty strong, though it was fading, and in some regions of the country it was already gone. But where I lived, you could still trust that a decent boy and girl could go on dates for years and not have to worry that they would get into trouble. Children—both boys and girls—delivered newspapers and collected their fees and tips once a month, and nobody was afraid that they would be beaten up or robbed. It is not just that people don't enjoy playing cards with a cheat. There is no point even bothering to try.

I mentioned before that, when I was an undergrad, the honor system was still strongly in force at Princeton. Because we were intelligent creatures, made in the image of God, it was taken for granted that we were capable, if not of sanctity, at least of recognizing objective good and evil, and of directing our courses accordingly, if but with fits and starts and many stumbles along the way. Because we were fallen creatures, it was taken for granted that without self-restraints and the considerable power of social approval and disapproval, we would go bad, fast. If we deny both of these things, we elevate ourselves in theory to the status of all-determining gods, while debasing ourselves in practice to the misery of cheats, sneaks, ruffians, knaves, and whores. Then there is nothing to do—so we seem to have agreed—but to submit to the massive and grossly ineffectual power of an all-invading bureaucratic state.

And that is the subject of our next chapter.

THE FIFTH LIE

The Foundation and the Fulfillment
of All Human Society Is Equality

I MAY ADD to the falsehood above the following corollary: whatever equality we do not find among human beings as they are naturally constituted, we will attempt to impose by force, and the only force capable even of beginning that task will be the massive and monstrous state, democratic in name, imperial in practice, irresponsible, and growing by means of its own failures.

If you ask me whether I "believe in equality," I must ask, "In what respect do you intend the term?"

I understand that Christians are supposed to "believe in equality," but I find it expressed in the New Testament only in certain relations, and among those, not necessarily the deepest or the highest. In Christ, says St. Paul to the Galatians, stubborn and prideful and ostentatiously submissive as they were, "there is neither Jew nor Greek, there is neither slave nor free, there is neither male nor female" (Gal. 3:28). That verse has been so construed as to level all hierarchical orders and social distinctions, so that critics have doubted whether the same St. Paul wrote the letter to the Ephesians, which notoriously insists upon subordination in the home and the Church, not noticing that Paul is *always* insisting upon subordination, even in the letters they cannot deny are genuinely his; or they say that Paul was muddled or was too timid to follow to their conclusion the revolutionary words he wrote above. That is to read Scripture in the hopes of finding yourself there, like the pool where the enraptured boy Narcissus found his own face, and fell in love with it, to his foolish and inevitable destruction.

It is an act of sheer temerity to attribute inconsistency to a genius, or cowardice to a man who was stoned, shipwrecked, flogged, imprisoned, and beheaded for what he believed in (cf. 2 Cor. 11:22–33); impiety to attribute it to someone who, as your church holds, was inspired by God to become the great apostle to the Gentiles, and to write the world-altering letters he wrote. The problem, in fact, is ours and not Paul's. We are the ones beholden to an egalitarian ideology. We want to take equality not as medicine for our fallen nature, as a guardrail against our taking evil advantage of one another, but as real food, and perhaps as the whole content of the heavenly feast. But equality is a mathematical, mechanical, legalistic, or juridical notion: as C. S. Lewis says, "Equality is a quantitative term and therefore love often knows nothing of it" (*The Weight of Glory*, "Membership"). Justice speaks its language, and must do so, in many though not all respects. Love, however, does not speak that language, for the lover revels in the excellence of the beloved, and in that reveling, love does not care to measure its own relative height. "It delights me," Lewis goes on to say, "that there should be moments in the services of my own Church when the priest stands and I kneel."

Inequality and the Body

St. Paul says that the Church is the "Body of Christ" — it is his most powerful metaphor, if it is a metaphor at all and not the revelation of a mysterious truth. He says so to the Corinthians, to allay the spirit of contention among them and to remind them that the same Holy Spirit works in each member of the body according to his will:

For just as the body is one and has many members, and
all the members of the body, though many, are one body,
so it is with Christ. For by one Spirit we were all baptized
into one body—Jews or Greeks, slaves or free—and all
were made to drink of one Spirit. For the body does not
consist of one member but of many. If the foot should say,
"Because I am not a hand, I do not belong to the body,"
that would not make it any less a part of the body. (1 Cor.
12:12–15)

There are, then, no degrees in Baptism. Keep in mind that Baptism,
by its very nature, no more admits of degrees than death and res-
urrection do. For Baptism is a ritual drowning; we are, says Paul,
baptized into Christ's death (Rom. 6:3). You cannot drown halfway;
you cannot drown one-half of yourself and not the other. Likewise,
you cannot be raised halfway from the dead. Lazarus did not come
from the tomb half alive and half rotting. The baptized member
of the body has been the recipient of a miracle of grace; and there
is no such thing as half a miracle, no more than there is schism in
Christ Himself. You can be a good Christian or a bad Christian.
You cannot be a half Christian, except by way of a figure of speech.

But if we take Paul's metaphor seriously, we see, first of all, a
diversity of persons and of gifts, and not sameness, and in this way
the realm of grace is founded upon and elevates the realm of nature,
for "to one is given through the Spirit the utterance of wisdom, and
to another the utterance of knowledge according to the same Spirit,
to another faith by the same Spirit, to another gifts of healing by
the one Spirit" (1 Cor. 12:8–9). I can do things that not one person
in ten thousand can do, perhaps not one in a hundred thousand.
But I cannot draw a human face that will not look like a cartoon,
and not a good cartoon at that. I could never have been more than

adequate on the piano. I can scramble and rearrange letters with astonishing speed and facility, and I can commit thousands of lines of poetry to memory, but I am bad at remembering people's names and faces (though excellent at remembering their voices), and I am clumsy at seeing how three-dimensional shapes can fit together.

And what of it? I am deeply grateful that there are people in the world who can draw and paint far better than I can, who take to musical instruments as easily as I take to languages and grammar and words, and who are as slow in speech and the social graces as they are speedy in inventing and operating machines. All these things are *gifts*, and as soon as we confess that they are gifts, we have admitted into our midst the fundamental, dynamic, and beautiful *inequality* between the giver of the gift and the receiver.

"We acknowledge the inequality between God and man," the egalitarians may say, "but that is the only inequality we admit as morally meaningful. We also acknowledge," they say, but grudgingly, "that intellectual and artistic talents are not spread evenly across the population. We hesitate to say that one gift is more valuable than another, and we affirm that such talents are in fact spread evenly across all nations and between both sexes. And we say that the aim of all social action must be to reduce inequalities, in wealth, political influence, and honor, as far as possible. This aim is good in itself, and is productive of peace, because it is inequality that gives rise to conflict, when one person has much and another has little." Actually, the reverse is true. Societies that accept inequalities in station as a matter of course tend to be peaceful, while those that demand equality must be in a state of constant turmoil, because a narrow-eyed envy supplants humility, and a nervous suspicion reigns among the rich, because they suspect that they do not deserve their wealth, and they are often right about that.

But let us turn to the naturalness of one most obvious inequality in human life. Must I go through the tiresome exercise of showing that when it comes to physical prowess, the inequality between a healthy man and a healthy woman is staggering? Thank God for the stopwatch. In the one land sport that rewards sheer brute strength and muscle mass the *least*—running—the advantage of males over females is still as wide as the Grand Canyon. Florida keeps copious statistics for each year's high school athletes in track and field. Every year, in each of the track events common to both, five or six *high school boys*, in that single state of Florida, which holds about 0.003 of the world's population, do better than the *all-time women's world records*. We are not talking about the same five or six speedsters, either, but about fifty or sixty boys scattered across the various events. No wonder: high school boys run faster than women—a lot faster. And when they get where they are running to, they bring far more strength. In that regard, there is no comparison. Boys' soccer teams have murdered women's World Cup teams; and again, that's just soccer, another sport that does not reward brute strength in the hands, arms, shoulders, chest, and back. Take any group of healthy men and women in the prime of life, doing physical labor every day. The strongest woman will still be overmatched by the weakest man. That is why Amish men, not Amish women, raise the barns and build the houses.

It is vital, this inequality. Without it, we could never have built up the technological civilization we take for granted, nor could we maintain it. We might put it this way: If men were only as strong as teenage boys, would they have had the strength to develop foundries, to dig for ore and stone, to hew the trees that built their houses and made their early machines, to lay down roads, or even to break horses and wrestle with large cattle, for plowing the fields? I doubt it. Boys can do a lot, but I think that the oak, a soggy stretch of land, earth as hard as brick when it is dry, and an unruly ox would break them first. If teenage boys couldn't do it, forget about their sisters and their mothers, who are not as strong as they are.

In our time, we can barely be permitted to notice this most obvious distinction between the sexes. But you don't have to be a committed evolutionist to see it and to suppose that without it, we would not be here to discuss it. The human child is utterly helpless, and even at age seven or eight would probably die in a few weeks if left to fend for himself in the wilds, regardless of the occasional "wolf-boy" here or there, or Mowgli of happy memory. That means he must be cared for, and with infants, it means continual attention and feeding from the breast. If women were as risk hungry as many men are, or as prone to abstractedness, or as restless in the body as the muscles cry out for action, their babies would suffer for it; nature would not reward it. But if men were not bigger and stronger than women, they could not serve as fit providers and protectors. The larger body costs a great deal in food and must justify itself by an even larger benefit in food. The more muscular body poses a great risk to the weaker woman and must justify itself by posing a far greater risk to predators, human or otherwise, and a far greater opportunity to take advantage of what nature offers. Hence the relations between man and woman have been characterized not by equality but by mutuality and inequality: the protector and provider, who stands guard at the periphery, acts *for the benefit* of the woman and child, and they in turn submit to his leadership. For their own sake, very few men will do anything at all beyond what is necessary to keep reasonably warm and fed. But if you see a well-appointed house with a garden, it is what a man has done for the woman he loves. In the order of governance, he is first; in the order of ends, she is first.

She must be first. For the woman is the bearer of new life. When the *Titanic* was sinking, women and children were given the first chance to board the lifeboats. That is not sentimentality. It is the prime *earthly* motive for any true man. Men are, as I have often written, indispensable in their being dispensable. The population of your tribe will not be determined by the number of men but by the number of women. Cut the number of women in half, and it will take you a very long time to return to your original population, if you ever do. Cut the number of men in half, and—think of tribes that practice polygamy—it will take you but a single generation. The imbalance here is colossal. The woman contributes years and years of her life, even her bodily substance, to the bearing and nursing of children, so that the man, to compensate, must contribute all he can with brain and brawn, by himself sometimes but most dynamically and productively with his brothers by blood or his brothers by the bonds of a common life, to the protection of and the provision for those most vulnerable and most valuable people. Left to his own devices, man would scrabble together a hand-to-mouth life; but he digs, he plows, he hews, he quarries, he builds, and he fights, both proximately and ultimately, for the families, that is, for the women and children, his own in the first instance, and everyone else's too.

So firmly is this imperative fixed in the mind of the good man that it extends to women beyond their child-bearing years, as it extends to crippled children who can never be of any *utilitarian* value to the society. Thus, all measures that bring some women into what must always remain essentially masculine-protective roles, such as fighting in war, are purchased by the attenuating of that imperative. Men, after all, will follow a premise to its logical conclusion. The premise that women and men make equally good soldiers leads inevitably to the conclusion that women do not merit protection by men. The premise is false, and the conclusion is disastrous. Nor is it logical to complain loudly that some bad men hurt women, when even bad men are far more likely to kill or to batter other men, and when you are putting women forward for the murderousness and hellishness of war. You have given up any warrant for that special consideration.

The man, then, is built to lead. We should not ask, "Why do men have deep voices and rough chins?" We should ask instead, "Why do women *not* have deep voices and rough chins?" The voice, the face, the glossiness of the smooth skin, the relative lack of muscle mass, all help to associate the woman with the child; and as you should never raise your fist in anger against a child, so should you never raise your fist in anger against a woman, regardless of the provocation. It is wrong.

We should suppose that such a strong directive would color the very attraction that is natural between boys and girls, men and women. Look at a photograph of a husband and wife, embracing. It does not matter how old they are, or how physically fit they are. The man is almost always taller—women do not prefer men who are shorter than they are—and he has broader shoulders, and the woman leans into him, as he wraps his arm around her shoulder or waist. Look at how men and woman dance. They do not dance as men dance *beside* other men, in the war whoops of the native Hawaiians or the acrobatic dance of the young Phaeacian lads before their guest, Odysseus, as they leap high in the air to a drumbeat and fling a ball back and forth. Men and women dance as equal unequals: as man for woman, and woman for man, each giving to the other, and what they give, equally in love, is not the same.

Inequality and the Mind

One of the most obvious features of human life is that we are not all possessed of the same mental acuity, and though we can speak, more or less definitely, about a general level of intelligence, it is not going to be expressible in every person in the same ways; literary genius does not imply mechanical genius, theoretical genius does not imply artistic genius.

I know no time when I did not know how to read. Nobody taught me. I picked it up, somehow. So my mother tells me. I can date the running comic strip I got up when I was a little boy, because it is interrupted by some strips describing my mother's going to the hospital, and that happened around my fifth birthday, when my brother was born. Had I not been burdened with school, as I see now, I might have been doing calculus at age twelve, or I might have learned several languages by then; I was a sponge for memory.

Schools are not set up for such a strange child as I was. They are set up for the great middle, and not to raise them up, but to keep them plodding along in a middling way. Hence the calamitous decision, in the 1930s, to deprive the child's hungry mind of the nutrition of many and new and difficult words, and hence also the severe segregation of children into grade levels, regardless of what they might accomplish if they were set free. We have purchased a broad equality at the expense of genius.

It is a terrible trade. We are apt to think, because we are individualists, that the cost is mainly borne by the most gifted people, who we suppose will be all right in the end; we need not worry too much about them. If by that we mean that they will likely get decent jobs, sure, that is not a thing to worry about. But if we mean that they will do the great work they otherwise would have done, I believe we are dead wrong, and that history will bear me out in this judgment.

I am thinking now of the boy Michelangelo, enrolled at a young age as an apprentice in the family studio of the master Florentine painter, Domenico Ghirlandaio. The studio was open only to boys and men, and before we turn away from it in moral disgust, I should like to point out that such studios were responsible for more great art, by far, than all our current university art departments put together. In any case, we should consider not only what practical skills the young Michelangelo learned there, regarding the mixing of paints, the production of certain colors and their properties, the preparing of wet plaster for frescoes, the blocking out of large figures on *cartoni* and their arrangement so as to form a coherent whole rather than a crowd of figures milling about and making the eye dizzy or weary—I am no artist, and I know of these things only distantly and in a vaguely general way. But the total intellectual import of Michelangelo's apprenticeship cannot be reckoned. He was embedded in a hierarchy of scholar-artists, overhearing their conversation, instructed in the many-faceted symbolism of Christian iconography that went back all the way to the catacombs. Greatness does not hoard itself up, though the *potential* for it can be smothered by dull routine or left inert by lack of opportunity. "Some mute inglorious Milton here may rest," says the poet Gray in his famous elegy as he walks through a country churchyard.

There is another threat to greatness, one that no one before the age of mass industrial production could have imagined. Before I name it, I would like to glance at one of the many novels by Sir Walter Scott that were once read by countless schoolboys in England and America: *Rob Roy.* Scott heads every chapter with a quotation from a poet or a playwright; a few, attributed to "Anonymous," may be his own. Chapter 30, wherein we are introduced to the fierce and formidable wife of the title character, begins with these lines from *Bonduca,* a Jacobean tragedy written two hundred years before Scott:

> General,
> Hear me, and mark me well, and look upon me
> Directly in my face—my woman's face;
> See if one fear, one shadow of a terror,
> One paleness dare appear, but from my anger,
> To lay hold on your mercies.

Pause, consider, evaluate. You are a schoolboy. Scott has brought you into the vicinity of a noble play (attributed to Shakespeare's younger contemporary and sometime collaborator, John Fletcher).

The lines above are of very high quality: blank verse, straightforward, no frills or nonsense about them. It seems that Bonduca herself is uttering them, and that, although she is a woman, she feels no fear. You wonder: "Where does this story come from?" It stays in your mind. Or perhaps you do recognize the name, though you never knew that a play was written about her, and you recall that a Celtic princess named Boadicea (d. 60/61) once led a bold rebellion against Rome, in a losing cause. You are being immersed in a world of stories and art, one that your author takes for granted; his own greatness invites you into that world. You learn, as it were, by proximity to greatness, and Scott is not such a miser as to make you focus on himself alone. Without your knowledge of it, as it were unconsciously but naturally, you are being taught and elevated. It is the quality of genius — and by no means do I suggest that that can be found only or even primarily in schools — to raise up the ordinary to heights they could not otherwise attain, or perhaps imagine.

Thus did many thousands of men over the course of five hundred years grace the landscapes of Europe with the most intricate and beautiful buildings ever formed by human hands. Some of them were the most accomplished of masters, no doubt, though we do not know their names; most were ushered into greatness by their willingness to be taught by, and led by, their superiors, and these men worked not as slaves but as fully engaged artists, stretched to the limits of their skill, as the second violinist is upraised by the composer, the conductor, and the first violinist who is his superior. Thus did many thousands of mere boys, in choirs in every church in Europe, contribute their essential part, and often the most salient part, in the realization of choral works composed for just such voices along with those of full-grown men. Thus did many thousands of people, in countless villages from Poland to Portugal, stage the popular dramas during the old three-day feast of Corpus Christi.

The magnificent raises the excellent, the excellent raises the fine, the fine raises the average. In the vicinity of recognized and celebrated greatness (in the vicinity of the Italian opera, let us say, and Italian painting and sculpture), the brothers Ernesto and Giambattista de Curtis, the former a composer and poet, the latter a poet, painter, playwright, and sculptor, born into a noble family—compose the Neapolitan art song "*Torna a Surriento*" ("Come Back to Sorrento"), which soon becomes one of the most popular songs in the nation; the youth with the mandolin in the piazza of any little town in Italy may be singing it, and so would be the local talent in the small opera houses that the Italians built in America and every other nation to which they emigrated. In the vicinity of recognized and celebrated greatness—in the vicinity of the national composers of other lands, George Gershwin writes *the* American opera, *Porgy and Bess*, inconceivable without Brahms and Dvořák, but also inconceivable without the long tradition of American folk songs and Negro spirituals, to which it is deeply indebted, and which it raised to the pinnacle of artistic achievement.

Little hills do not inspire the ambition to climb; mountains do. The Soviets themselves, their better instincts running athwart their egalitarian ideology, kept the Bolshoi Ballet a thing to amaze the world, which they could do only by means of hierarchical structures, and by acknowledging the worth of genius. A Nureyev comes perhaps once in a century. But the worst threat to genius was not engineered by the Soviets. It has been engineered, perhaps unwittingly, by the very successes of Western wealth. When Walter Scott wrote, there was no such thing as a paperback, and mass-produced fluff or garbage was not yet possible. But it is certainly possible now. We are suffocated with it. It is not just that it is hard to find the gems among an interminable output of glass beads. That is bad enough. It is also that the very idea of a gem has faded; we do not know that we should be looking for the gems; and if we do know that we should be looking for them, we have no clear idea of what we are looking for, and how to tell it apart from the glass. Meanwhile, the glass—the ordinary, the average—has itself sagged in quality, so that most of what otherwise would be glass is but shiny plastic.

It may be objected that I am beholden to an optical illusion. Most of the bad stuff that any age will produce will be forgotten, like the "*cacata carta*" of the worthless poet Catullus satirizes (*Carmina*, 36.1); I do not think I need to translate his epithet. But I think instead that people who charge me with the optical illusion are themselves suffering from an optical illusion. They assume that the quantity and the quality of the forgettable things that our age produces are about on par with those of the productions of past ages. I do not think that the evidence bears them out. When I read popular magazines of more than a hundred years ago, I find greatness mingled with good, solid, worthwhile, intelligent matter, just as, if you rummage about in antique furniture, you may find a Chippendale in the midst of solid, handsome, well-made tables and chairs. What you don't find is trash; no one could afford to make trash, and no one could afford to purchase it. Moreover, the excellent set a visible standard. Look at public buildings in the United States erected before 1900: banks, department stores, town halls, churches. You would not call them all great works of art. Most made no such claim. But they please the eye and the mind, and they are likewise and for many of the same reasons comfortable to the human body. Why, a prison like the state penitentiary in Cranston, Rhode Island, is far more handsome to behold, more pleasing in its shape and its severe but still visible adornment, than most *churches* are now.

Our political conversation is not led by the wisest voices, by men and women of broad experience and moral probity, but by the shrill noises of crowds and those who play up to them. Wisdom and sloganeering are not good friends. In short order, even the wise become demagogues. When they are covered in mud, an Adonis and a Quasimodo look much the same. When they are surrounded by noise, Heifetz and your nephew who scrapes a violin string as a cat may scrape a blackboard sound much the same. In a glut of words, Shakespeare's "Let me not to the marriage of true minds / Admit impediments" (*Sonnets*, 116.1–2) can hardly be uttered, because no one will wait long enough for an intelligent sentence to end. And all the evils of the mass phenomena are, I say, exacerbated by the lie, that there is no aristocracy of mind, or that there *should be* none.

Inequality of Ends

Suppose you were given these choices. You could live entirely content, like a well-fed pig, to a ripe old age of a hundred years, but you would know nothing profound, and do nothing particularly good, enjoy no depths of love, and embark on no noble adventure. Or you could live a relatively short life, marked with times of profound suffering, taking your chances — I will guarantee nothing at all. What human being would not choose to be a real human being, rather than the well-fed pig?

Much of Homer's *Odyssey* is predicated on an inequality of ends. When the boy Telemachus shows up at the house of his father's old friend and comrade in arms, Menelaus, he is amazed by the man's wealth, and it is certainly true that Menelaus treats him well. We do not doubt the old warrior's sincerity. When he says that he loved and admired Odysseus best of all his comrades, we believe him. But we notice, too, that things are not quite right with this man surrounded by gold and silk and thoroughbred horses, not to mention Helen, the most beautiful woman in the world. Menelaus says much about what he *would do or would have done* to help Odysseus, and we do not doubt that if the occasion presented itself before him, he would be as good as his word. He is not a liar, and he is not a coward. But what you would do, and what you will do or have done, are not the same things. Menelaus *would have* avenged the murder of his brother, Agamemnon, but as it turned out, because he had spent so much time trading in Egypt, he returned to Sparta only on the very day that Agamemnon's son Orestes, finally growing to manhood, avenged his father's death by slaying the usurper Aegisthus and his confederate, Agamemnon's wife—Helen's own sister—Clytemnestra. Menelaus will be numbered among the immortals, but only on account of his marriage with the god-begotten Helen. Time and again, in fact, he is made subordinate to Helen, and not always to his own or anybody else's benefit, as when the good woman slips him and Telemachus a drug so that they will not weep, as they think about Odysseus, the friend and the father they fear they have lost. That last trick is quite the opposite of what Odysseus himself will do, when he is feasting with his royal hosts in Phaeacia, and he calls upon the blind poet Demodocus to sing what he knows very well will cause him to weep—to sing a song about the Trojan War.

Comfort, then, is a mean end, when compared with the courage, the endurance, and the risk-taking of the true man. We see it also when Odysseus and his men are becalmed on the island where the cattle of the sun god Helios are browsing. They have been warned not to touch those cattle. But when their provisions have run out, and they grow sick of trying to ease their hunger with a scrawny fish or two, and when Odysseus, having retired into the island to pray to the gods for help and to look for food, is no longer around them to brace their courage or to threaten them with death if they should disobey him, they give in; they must eat. Homer calls them out at the very beginning of the poem. They are *nepioi*, he says, "ninnies."

Gratifying the flesh, too, is a mean end, when compared with the social and the intellectual ends of man. The suitors who have swarmed upon Odysseus's estate and are slaughtering his cattle for their feasts are well-spoken, well-dressed, naturally intelligent people. The Cyclops, Polyphemus, who treats Odysseus's plea for hospitality with brutish contempt, slaying and devouring one of his men for an evening and a morning snack, is ill-spoken, crudely dressed, and rather dim in the intellectual marquee. But the suitors and the Cyclops have a lot in common. They do not use their brains to think of what is right, and even their attempts at cunning fail them. They also do not meet with others of their kind to pursue the common good. Ithaca, without its king Odysseus, has not had a public assembly in almost twenty years, as is noted when Telemachus, now having come of age, calls its citizens together to appeal to their moral intelligence, and to have them relieve his household of the suitors who are oppressing it. But the people of Ithaca do not take any action, partly because of the brute threats that one of the ringleaders, Eurymachus, levels at an aged prophet who predicts that Odysseus will return. The message is clear: we are many, we are young, and we will do as we please. In that sense, they are no different from the Cyclops. He is big, Odysseus and his comrades are small, and he will do as he pleases. And it does not please the Cyclops and his fellows to meet in assembly. We think they are brutish because of the single big eye they have in the middle of the forehead. Well, it is not a pleasant thing to look at. But if you want a more cogent expression of their not rising to the full stature of a human being, look no farther than their self-isolation. "They lord it over their wives and children," says Odysseus, in his last word on the character of these creatures, "and no one has to do with anyone else" (*Odyssey*, 9.114–115).

I am well aware that many people will balk at assigning a scale of values to the things we choose to do. But the moral reality is organized in such a way. We pretend to doubt it only when the shoe pinches our corns, and we must acknowledge that we have spent our efforts on lesser ends than those that should have stirred our souls. Of course, it is impossible always to be aiming at great things. We must relax, or we will go mad. We must attend to small things too. But if you said you wish to be wealthy so that you can spend all your days watching television and playing solitaire, we would look upon you as stunted, as a tree that is hunched and thin and splitting in the bark and bearing little or no fruit. The ends you have chosen are unworthy of the kind of being you are. We cannot always be reading great books, just as we cannot always be eating rich food. Sometimes we need the sustenance and the nourishment of what is good and solid, like roast beef and potatoes. But in any case, we should not be starving ourselves of what is good and solid; we should not be eating garbage.

An inequality of ends suggests also a *hierarchy of ends*, and this, too, is undeniable, if you are honest and you consider the matter. John wishes to marry Sally because he loves her and he believes he will be happy, and she will be happy, if they live together for the rest of their lives. But if John said, "What I really need is to feel happy, so that I can marry Sally," we would not condemn him so much as wonder whether he had lost his senses. The statement seems absurd, as if you were to say that you were going to go for a walk so that you could put your old shoes on — not new shoes, because you might just be trying them out, and then your statement could make sense. Animals act with an immediate end: the dog chases the squirrel, and if he's a wild dog, he chases it so that he can catch it and eat it. Human beings, though, often act for distant ends, distant not simply in time but in the order of desirability. John goes to the swimming pool to swim a mile or two of laps. He doesn't mind it, but he doesn't really enjoy it either. He does it so that he will lose a little weight and tone up his muscles. He's not vain, but he thinks that if he were more physically fit, he might be more attractive to Sally. After all, he is falling in love with her. He thinks he might want to marry her—and if he is right about it, that will make him happy. The actions are ordered to an end, one that is desirable in itself: in this case, the end that is happiness.

John may be mistaken about any step in his reasoning. Sally might not care how he looks. Sally might not be the right woman for him to marry. She might not be a good woman for any man to marry; we don't know. But there is no irresistible instinct in John to go to that swimming pool. He reasons, and practical reason proceeds always to some end that is considered desirable in itself, even if we do not spell it out so in our minds.

Well and good, you may say, but what does it matter? Plato can instruct us here. The city is like a body—we do call it the "body politic"—and the individual man, host to many desires and the originator of many thoughts, is like a city or a state, and indeed is sometimes like a city in the midst of civil upheaval or war. The body is healthy only if the ends of its members are subordinated to the good of the whole, which good also redounds to the good of the members since you cannot have a perfectly healthy organ in a radically unhealthy body. Now, the lie of egalitarianism—I am, again, not speaking of the ontological equality of human persons, nor am I speaking of egalitarian measures that are prudentially embraced in a society for the sake of the rights of individuals and the common good—is that you can have social order or order within the human soul without acknowledging that some things are nobler than others, and that some minds are clearer and cleaner than others. Where everyone considers himself a leader, there are no leaders at all but a self-willed mob. Where everyone considers himself entitled to press his opinions on the world, regardless of his learning or his practical experience, you have no discussions but shouting. American elections are now just shouting matches, and they have long been so, because the alternative would require people to be quiet, to listen, to think, perhaps to take time to read, and certainly to set their own desires, always tending to be clamorous and distracting, to the side.

One of the evil results of the shouting match is that nobody can conceive of taking collective and public action now so as to attain a great but distant and uncertain end, and nobody inquires into how a single bad principle can lead to distant but disastrous results. We have lost our capacity to be socially and intellectually architectonic. Think of the medieval craftsmen who worked at building a cathedral that they themselves would never see completed. Think of the hundreds of things, great and small, that must be ordered in the construction of such an edifice to produce the intended result: for you do not lay a proper foundation unless you already have the completion in mind. The theologians, master builders, masons, carpenters, glaziers, sculptors, and others—even the men who hewed the great trees in the forests for beams to span the interior spaces—could not have taken a single step without a hierarchy of persons governing a hierarchy of ends.

A democracy, of itself, cannot produce statesmen like Webster and Calhoun; I am speaking here not of the justice of their aims but of the *kind* of men they were. Only forces that resist the leveling tendencies of democracy can do that. The alternative is to give the day to the people leading the forces that shout the loudest, sometimes shouting with guns, but almost always shouting with condemnations, threats, ridicule, making themselves and their adherents and their targets less and less likely to reason about anything. Reason, by its nature hierarchical, must rule, or force will rule in its place.

Leadership?

One of the strangest things about our current egalitarian language is that we prattle at the same time about "leadership," which we wish to extend to everyone. Go to the website of any school or college, and you will be regaled with lies about how the students will all be taught to be "leaders." A moment's thought is sufficient to explode the lie. If everyone is a leader, then there are no leaders at all, because no one is following. By definition, leaders must be rare.

For any particular purpose you set forth, most people are simply incapable of leading others to attain it, because they lack the intelligence, or the skills, or the farsightedness, or the gift of inspiring others to follow their vision and make it their own. But that does not mean that we should retire in sullenness from the leader's direction. *Obedience is the virtue whereby the inferior shares in the authority of the superior.* I do not mean compliance but true obedience, which, as the etymology of the word suggests, implies *hearing and heeding.* "I shall walk at liberty," says the psalmist in one of the most exalted and perspicacious poems of obedience, "for I have sought thy precepts" (Ps. 119:45). It is a joy to him, not a burden. "Oh, how I love thy law!" he cries. "It is my meditation all the day" (119:97).

I have long considered the relation of a father to a grown son, plying the same trade. The good father, says Charles Péguy, wants his son to be stronger than he is, even if that means that the father will eventually be forgotten in the village: "And when they'll say his name in town, when they talk about him, when his name gets brought up in conversation, as it happens, it won't be him they're talking about but his sons" (*The Portal of the Mystery of Hope*). It is what the noble Hector says when he dandles his baby son, Astyanax: let the Trojans say the son is far better than his father was, when they see him come blood-stained from battle (*Iliad*, 6.479–480). Aeneas wants the same for his son Iulus, for whose sake alone he leaves Troy, burning to the ground at the hands of the victorious Greeks. Virgil, the poet of the *Aeneid*, once he has led the pilgrim Dante to the peak of the mountain of Purgatory, tells him that he has reached the limit of his instruction. "Take your own pleasure for your leader now" (*Purgatorio*, 27.131), says the poet who has given all he had for the welfare of one he regards not just as a fellow poet and a friend but as a beloved son. Odysseus returns to Ithaca, wondering who has remained loyal to him and his house. He has few doubts about his wife Penelope, but what can he imagine about his son Telemachus, who was only a baby when Odysseus set out for Troy nearly twenty years before? But the boy, growing into his stature as a man, shows all the family nobility and courage, and not only does he fight beside his father, at Odysseus's direction; he dares to tell his father that one feature of his plan—that is, to visit and to test the tenant farmers, in disguise, one by one before he goes to the main house—would take too much time, and were best left for afterwards. And Odysseus, the father, agrees. What a fine thing it must be for father and son to confer on equal-unequal terms about some great work to be done! And if the son gives good counsel, the father nods, smiles, is proud, and says, "We'll do it that way, then," making the decision, and thus does the father's authority, his giving of increase, his making-greater, take root in the obedient son and come to full flourishing.

Or consider the telling words of the centurion, who pleads with Jesus to heal the servant he loves like a son. When Jesus offers to go to the man's house—and keep in mind, the man is likely a pagan, a soldier in the Roman army, so that to enter his house would render Jesus ritually unclean—the centurion stops him. "I am not worthy that you should come under my roof," he says. Jesus need but speak the word, and his servant shall be healed. "I am a man under authority," says this leader of a hundred soldiers, "and I say to one, 'Go,' and he goes, and to another, 'Come,' and he comes, and to my slave, 'Do this,' and he does it" (Matt. 8:9). The centurion is worthy to lead because he himself obeys. We are not talking about blind and stupid obedience in what is wicked; there is no sense of that in the text.

Shakespeare, too, was well aware of the role obedience plays in leadership. It is everywhere in his plays. An entire theory of human society is given dramatic form in the sudden and terrific opening scene of *The Tempest*. You are sitting in the theater, the curtain is drawn, and—thunder and lightning! And the master of the ship calls to the boatswain, calling him "Good" (1.1.3), and giving him orders to relay to the mariners, because they are in danger of being blown too near the rocky shore, and thus being dashed to pieces. The boatswain, a hearty fellow, cries to the mariners in turn, "Cheerly, my hearts!" (5). They must take the mainsail down, and "tend to the Master's whistle!" (6). Think: in the hurly-burly of the storm, the master's voice cannot be heard. He must give his instructions in the code of a piercing whistle, and the boatswain and the mariners, listening for them and heeding them, must be on the spot, "yare," "ready," prompt to obey, lest they all perish. If the ship sinks, the men whose job it is to sail her will not have been to blame. Meanwhile, the noblemen whom the mariners have aboard, including their very king, come out on deck to remonstrate with them, but the boatswain will have none of it. "You mar our labor!" he cries (13)—they are getting in the way of his and his mariners' duties; they are distracting them; their cries are louder than the storm. When the king himself says, "Where is the Master?" the boatswain replies with a sturdy incredulity, "Do you not hear him?" (12–13). And that refers both to the whistle and to the storm itself, which is the work of God. "Out of our way, I say!" he cries (27), when a brace of noblemen lesser than the king—sinful men all three, by the way—begin to curse him for not knowing his place. The irony is that the boatswain *does know his place, and they do not know theirs*: it is their duty now to obey, as the boatswain himself obeys.

"Ah, but we teach our students *to lead themselves*," say the egalitarians, grasping at a straw. Lay not that flattering unction to your souls, you egalitarians. Lemmings of Tomorrow, I have called such people, leading themselves all by obeying the promptings of mass phenomena, as they hurtle over the cliff into the sea. We must obey. We will either obey the God who, as St. Paul says, desires sons, not slaves (Gal. 4:7), so that the more ardently we obey Him, the more liberty we enjoy, or, pretending to obey ourselves, we really obey the deceiver, who was "a murderer from the beginning," "a liar and the father of lies" (John 8:44). "Here at least / We shall be free," says Milton's Satan, as he beholds for the first time the dismal reaches of Hell, his prison-house (*Paradise Lost*, 1.258–259). "I am my own," Dante's Satan, mute and shackled in ice, appears to say with every robotic flap of his wings, raising the gale that freezes the sluggish Cocytus to lock him in place forever. If only he could cease to tell that lie, the Cocytus would melt, and he might be able to move an inch or two. But the lie is what he is, self-deceived, self-led, self-misled.

In practice, they who will not obey God and who scoff at legitimate authority will be easy prey to the demagogue, the confidence man, the swindler, and the pimp, and in case none is at hand to pinch their noses and pull them along, they themselves will do the favor. Alienated from God, the Russian people were reduced to honoring the hate-filled destroyer Lenin as a saint, and, as if that were not bad enough, they ended up paying homage to Stalin the mass murderer, Papa Joe, even while plenty of influential atheists, sipping tea at the headquarters of the *Daily Worker* or burrowing like moles in the departments of state in London and Washington, looked to him as a father leading the world into a brilliant and glorious laborer's paradise. The buffoonery of the wise who will not obey God! W. E. B. DuBois, a man of tremendous intelligence and depth of reading, was so far self-deceived that he wrote an obituary for Stalin (in the *National Guardian*, March 16, 1953) that would have brought a blush to the cheek of the most toadying flatterer the world has ever seen. "He knew the common man," writes DuBois, "felt his problems, followed his fate." That would *not* include the common man who worships God, or whose families had made of the Ukraine a breadbasket for Europe. Of the worship, DuBois expresses mild contempt, and as for the Ukrainian kulaks, the millions that Stalin murdered or reduced to starvation count in the tyrant's *favor*:

> The poor Russian peasant was the lowest victim of tsarism, capitalism and the Orthodox Church. He surrendered the Little White Father easily; he turned less readily but perceptibly from his ikons; but his kulaks clung tenaciously to capitalism and were near wrecking the revolution when Stalin risked a second revolution and drove out the rural bloodsuckers.

It never occurs to DuBois to wonder about life in a police state such as Ivan the Terrible would have loathed, let alone the mild and gently liberal Nicholas II, or whether the Orthodox Church meant more to the common people than simply providing a refuge for their misery, or whether "the rural bloodsuckers" were not correct, as the Ukraine would lie fallow, with weeds growing where wheat should have been, because tending the soil requires intelligence and long experience, and it is not bound to respect anyone's political fantasies.

Tastes in buffoonery change from age to age, but the essential thing remains. We don't take our buffoonery now, our slavish antics, in such masculine form as what we find in DuBois. It isn't vodka we drink, but soft drinks with sparkles, so that now it is the ridiculous drag queen who holds the day, prancing and wiggling his hips and mimicking every single stereotype of female behavior that the feminists themselves once rejected in contempt; but when it comes to self-imprisonment and the destruction of ordered liberty, no sacrifice is too great, and so the egalitarians fall to their knees in worship.

You must obey. The only choice is whom, or what. But surely we are progressing toward a society rich and tolerant enough to permit everyone to follow his own bent, from wherever it derives? His own bent will, I might say. But that lie, the lie of progress, raises its head to roar and to drown out all I have said till now. You, dragon, you are next in our sights.

THE SIXTH LIE

Cultural Progress Is Inevitable

OR, AS THE saying goes, you'd better get on "the right side of history."

The odd thing is that most people have believed in cultural decay rather than in cultural progress. At least the believers have been evenly matched. For every Roman expression of mere tolerance for their rude ancestors who did not know better, you will find an expression of dismay for current decadence. Livy (59 BC–AD 17) prefaces his great history of Rome by telling the reader of his intent, to show "the way of life and the customs that used to be, and the men and their arts that brought Roman rule to birth and gave it increase," until that stern discipline began to fall away, little by little at first, and then more and more, and quite headlong, "until we have at last arrived at these times, when we can no longer endure our vices nor their remedy." Livy began writing his history in 27 BC or shortly thereafter, and he worked on it regularly for the rest of his life. The times he is speaking of as his own were indeed fractious. Rome had been in the grip of civil conflict for a hundred years, and in the end there remained mostly the trappings of republican government, while the real power rested in the hands of an emperor. In Livy's time, that was the cold-hearted, ruthless, far-seeing, and eminently capable Augustus Caesar. But Rome would not always be so fortunate in that regard. The sour-tempered Tiberius followed upon Augustus, and then came Gaius, nicknamed Caligula or "Little Boots" when he was a boy following his father Germanicus in the military camps. Nero was yet to come; and though Rome did enjoy the rule of five consecutive good emperors, from Nerva through Marcus Aurelius (AD 96–180), she would also endure a long period in which almost all of her rulers held power for only a very short time, as assassination became the regular way of replacing one with another. And then came more than a century of economic stagnation, and waves of Germanic tribes invading the empire.

As the year 1000 was about to break, many Christians thought it might herald the end of the world. Optimists you will always have among you. Even when the year passed and the fire did not come, we find the great bishop Wulfstan, advisor to kings, a law-writer and administrator, and a man who had eyes to see what was going on around him, beginning a homily to the English people in these words: "My dear men, know the truth! This world is hastening to its end, and the longer it goes on the worse it gets, and it must needs be so, on account of the sins of the people, growing in evil before the coming of the Antichrist." Wulfstan wasn't just blowing smoke. King Edward, he recalls, "was betrayed and then slain, and his body burned," and then King Aethelred "was driven out of his country," leaving the Danes in control, and England in moral and social chaos; and Wulfstan is quite specific about the evils roundabout him, including the shocking rape, by "ten or twelve men, one after the other," Vikings all, of a thane's wife or daughter or kinswoman, while he is made to look on. Or "two or three sailors will drive herds of Christian men, all huddled together, from sea to sea about the country, to shame us before the whole world, if we are still capable of understanding any shame" (*Sermo Lupi ad Anglos*).

Jesus Himself does not say that the world will grow better and wiser with the passage of time. Rather the crisis will come, and "nation will rise against nation, and kingdom against kingdom," while the people themselves shall be unaware, for "as were the days of Noah, so will be the coming of the Son of man. For as in those days before the flood they were eating and drinking, marrying and giving in marriage, until the day when Noah entered the ark, and they did not know until the flood came and swept them all away, so will be the coming of the Son of man" (Matt. 24:7, 37–39). "Woe to those who dwell on the earth"! cries one of the angels of the apocalypse (Rev. 8:13).

"But the world is still with us," one may say, and what the myopic atheist Steven Pinker calls "the better angels of our nature" have come to the fore, and we do not murder as often as we used to, or rape, or pillage, and so forth. Progress, then. Let us examine the matter more closely.

The End Is Coming

The first thing I wish to note is that the Western idea of historical progress—quite foreign to the ways of thought that characterized classical China, Japan, and India, which emphasized stability, or only such change as you see in a turning wheel that yet does not advance—does not come, in the first instance, from the scientific revolution. It comes rather from the same eschatological springs that once moved Wulfstan to urge his fellow Englishmen to repent of their sins, for the world about them was falling apart. In a sense, it is not just the same kind of mind that seizes enthusiastically upon visions of imminent collapse or imminent glory, but that often one and the same person believes in both; and whether it is collapse or glory depends upon what feature of the situation he is regarding.

Dante, for example, was influenced by the prophetic and mystical writings of the Cistercian monk Joachim of Flora (d. 1202), who interpreted the book of Revelation as revealing the dawn of the "third age," the age of the Holy Spirit, when men would live in contemplative peace, and the Jews and the pagans would be converted. The year was to be 1260, and though that cataclysm did not occur, the abbot's theories continued to exert some influence. Dante has St. Peter, pitched to a holy rage by the corruption of the papacy at the time the poet attributes to his sacred pilgrimage (1300, and the sitting pope was Dante's inveterate enemy, Boniface VIII), cry out against it, predicting a cleansing soon to come:

> But that deep providence will aid us now—
> I see it coming—that defended Rome
> for the world's glory, raising Scipio.
> (*Paradiso*, 27.61–63)

Beatrice herself, Dante's guide through Heaven till almost the end, engages in the same kind of apocalyptic prophecy, setting it in the context of a history long enough to have accumulated a great discrepancy between the Julian calendar and the true solar year:

> But the neglected hundredths of your years
> won't make your January start in spring
> before these highest rings will shed such rays
> As will storm down the fortune you await,
> turning the prow and aft wholly about,
> so that the fleet a-sea will furrow straight,
> And, from the flower, the tree will bear good fruit.
> (27.142–148)

That marriage of reforming zeal and apocalyptic vision not only persisted into the Protestant Reformation; it became one of its leitmotifs. When the Elizabethan poet Edmund Spenser, in *The Faerie Queene*, casts the Catholic Church as the whore of Babylon—in the person of Duessa, the temptress and witch who attempts to displace

Una, the true Church, in the heart of the Red Cross Knight—he is not just wagging a finger at prelates behaving themselves badly. He really does see the battle as a cosmic one, involving the whole of Christian history, so that when the Red Cross Knight, freed from Duessa's bonds and cleansed of his own sin and folly, slays the dragon that has been besetting Una's parents and their kingdom, it is an event that unites the beginning of man with his end. For the realm is Eden, and Una's father, the king, is named Adam.

Some combination of social and ecclesial reformation inspired the fervor of many of the early splinter groups in the Reformation. There was, for example, a resurgence of the ancient Adamite movement; its adherents claimed to have regained the innocence lost in Eden, so they liked to go about naked, even in their worship. Madness, you say? Apocalypticism of the optimistic or the pessimistic variety does breed it. Consider the madman in John Webster's *The Duchess of Malfi* (1623):

> First Madman. Doomsday not come yet? I'll draw it nearer with a perspective [i. e., a magnifying glass], or make a glass shall set all the world on fire in an instant. I cannot sleep, my pillow is stuffed with a litter of porcupines. (4.2.73–75)

And one of his fellows:

> Third Madman. Greek is turned Turk; we are only to be saved by the Helvetian translation [i.e., by the Calvinist Bible from Geneva]. (85–86)

These are harmless men shut up in a madhouse, but the Levelers, so called by their enemies, were not shut up; they were an important force in the English Civil War, demanding the leveling of ancient distinctions of rank, and a broadly democratic view of both church and state. They had predecessors in leveling, for example in the Anabaptist revolt in Münster (1533–1535), where the charismatic leader John of Leiden took sixteen wives—polygamy being an oddly recurrent feature of enthusiastic movements intending to usher mankind into a great new future; see the careless and shallow promiscuity of men and women in Aldous Huxley's *Brave New World*, but also the more high-minded polygamy of the early Mormons, proclaiming themselves prophets, "Latter-Day Saints," for a new age and a new world.

Quakers, Shakers, Saint-Simonians, Fourierists, Christian Scientists, utopianists of all sorts, including Francis Bacon in *The New Atlantis*, all bear certain marks of family resemblance:

They believe that human history is going somewhere identifiable.

They believe they are in the forefront of the movement.

They believe that ancient modes of thought, including fundamental pieties, are being surpassed, and should therefore be discarded. That includes the Aristotelian philosophy of nature that Bacon vehemently rejected.

They view with suspicion all social structures, believing that they have come into existence by virtue of temporary conditions and necessities, not by the results of natural human activity.

Change, not stability, is the watchword.

Human history then neatly sorts out its saints and villains, characterized not so much by their personal piety or goodness but by their holding "advanced" or "outworn" political, social, economic, scientific, and religious opinions.

Some external event is looked upon as providing the crucial impetus for the leap forward, or its consummation: the supposed rediscovery of ancient Christianity, buried under more than a thousand years of superstition; the dethronement of Aristotle and Ptolemy by the new theories of celestial movement; the storming of the Bastille; the discovery of the New World; the establishment of John Winthrop's Puritan "city on a hill" to shine as a beacon for all the world; the burst of technological discovery and invention in the nineteenth century; the French Revolution and its enthronement of "Reason"—we can go on and on. Hitler's Third Reich; Mao's Cultural Revolution and its bloody attempt to obliterate the "Four Olds"; John Dewey's rejection of classical methods of education in favor of what he preached as the more scientific and democratic approach; the Wilsonian war to end all wars, the United Nations seen not as a bureaucratic wrench in the machinery of military aggression (which it has not proved to be, in any case) but as a seed of what the world must eventually become; the "giant leap for mankind" when Neil Armstrong set the first human foot on the surface of the moon, proving great impetus for science-fiction fantasies but, fifty years later, no apparent advance at all in human affairs—these are not so much the results of considered thought, as its mode and manner; not so much what we conclude, but the well-worn grooves of what we think about in the first place and how we think about it.

It was not Charles Darwin who invented the idea of "evolution," a word he disliked and rarely used. That idea was everywhere to be found, and it found a most convenient and food-rich host in Darwin's biological and archaeological theories. We should note that Darwin did not make the mistake of attributing any *end* to this evolution. It was not that marmosets and field mice were *better* than dinosaurs. It was merely that they happened to be better fit for the circumstances in which they and the elder creatures found themselves. Herbert Spencer and his followers, they were the popular preachers of evolution, using the biological theory as a springboard for social and political theories, or, with less reason but more enthusiasm, often of the bloody kind, for social and political action.

Have Moral Truths Evolved?

The short answer, approved by pagans from Plato and Cicero in the West to Lao-Tzu and Mencius in the East, is no, moral truths have not evolved. Whether mankind's apprehension of absolute and unchanging moral truths sharpens as the ages go on is another question. But first let me turn the evolutionist's reasoning itself *against* the notion that we may safely and cheerfully dispense with what our grandparents held to be true, because we are on the side of moral progress.

Scratch the surface of an ordinary pessimist and you may well find a lover of mankind, too much involved in the suffering of ordinary people to paste a smile upon it and go his way, whistling. The pessimist, not holding the future in awe, will be inclined to make the best of man as he finds him, grateful that things are no worse. Scratch the surface of an ordinary optimist and you will usually find a misanthrope, because man simply will not conform to his dreams of a glorious and usually conveniently vague future. The virtues of the pessimist are patience and forbearance; his vice may be sluggishness in undertaking reforms where those are possible and desirable. The virtue of the optimist is (a sometimes superficial) cheerfulness and a promptness in undertaking reforms; his vices are impatience, intolerance, and ingratitude.

Now then, the one thing in the world that most threatens the progressive optimist in the realizing of his dreams is man himself—man, recalcitrant, stubborn, forgetful, prone to vice, proud, envious, and double-hearted. If the optimist would but look in the mirror, he would see so much *there* to be reformed, or to beg God's grace in reforming, that he would hardly have time to pester his neighbor to death. But he does not look in the mirror. And when he looks at the world, and he sees that man has attained a degree of wealth that relieves almost all of the evolutionary pressure against vice and stupidity, he frets that *there will be too many of the wrong kinds of people*, and that is why he wishes to take man's biological and demographic future into his own hands, peddling contraception to the lower classes and using the schools not as places where young persons are taught the hard-won wisdom of their ancestors, but as recruitment centers for the great universal cause, the moral and social leap forward.

The people who first peddled the latex sheaths were usually puritan in their sensibilities. Their aim was not to spread vice but to curtail births—the wrong births. Theodore Roosevelt and Woodrow Wilson, the progressive Republican and the progressive Democrat, were both friendly to the idea of eugenics, though quite hostile to any effeminate relaxation of sexual mores. Roosevelt's good friend, the novelist and essayist Owen Wister, once twitted him for his old-fashioned mores, because he would not greet Maxim Gorky when he came to visit America—Gorky had an invalid wife, so he took a mistress. But you cannot peddle contraception without peddling vice, and this was especially the case once the Pill had been invented. Therefore, vice had to be rebranded as virtue, and the sluggish and ill-thought-out and craven following along with the vice must be regarded as bold and shrewd. You aren't tumbling off a precipice as long as you say you've done it on purpose, and you name it "ascent" and "advance."

If we look at the state of affairs, though, with the cold eye of an evolutionary theorist, we see straightaway that the pragmatic pressures that once taught people honesty, sexual continence, and integrity are gone, *with no demographic or immediate and obvious cultural penalty* for societies that abrogate those virtues. Hunger will teach the farmer to be sedulous, if nothing else will. In the villages of old, where everyone knew everyone else, dishonest dealing earned you the cold shoulder, and that was intolerable. When every child about to be born poses an appreciable danger to the mother's life, and when nobody wants to sweat out the last barely arable portions of a field to support some other man's child, people learn to keep their trousers and their skirts on until they get married—occasional escapades with a certain profession of women notwithstanding. If the storms come and wash out a bridge, your men must set about rebuilding it immediately. They must have more than the skills to do it. They must have the willingness; they must see it as their duty. If the neighbors are felled by smallpox or scarlet fever, their children must be seen to, and that duty falls upon the women. I am not derogating from the moral value of their actions if I note that they must understand that the treatment they give to their neighbors and townsmen will be theirs in return.

We are now, however, rich enough to afford every vice imaginable. Experience, that hard teacher when the pupil ignores the gentler counsel of wisdom, is either absent from the field or has turned coat and joined the noisy ragtag platoons of vice. If you are going to hold to the moral law *now*, you will often find yourself lonesome or despised or treated with remarkable indifference. Politicians have always, as a class, been a step or two away from confidence men and whores, but where is the pragmatic pressure now to keep them honest? The profligate man does not like to look at his bank statement, and vicious people do not like to be reminded of the virtues they do not possess. When was the last time a politician resigned, willingly, for the good of the body politic, because the mere whiff of dishonesty, of profit from a conflict of interest, of bartering influence for money, like dung at a banquet, would spoil the moral tenor of the enterprise? We have come to elect our politicians not for staid and boring old virtues but for their vices, their promotion of our vices, and their sales pitches. They are what the Italians used to call *ciarlatani*, "chatterers," mountebanks—the word means that they get up on a bench to address the crowds — selling the elixirs that their gaffs, the pollsters, have determined that the people want to buy.

By the criterion of the evolutionists themselves, by the measure of a success and failure with considerable consequences either way, it is wholly unreasonable to suppose that we are now *gaining* in moral wisdom. Wealth has spoiled many a child. Our wealth is like an inattentive and careless parent.

Are We Better Anyhow?

But have our morals improved in fact, regardless of the lack of pressure? Here we need to be careful, because human affairs are always quite a tangle. Rarely does a society sag in *all* moral respects. The century that saw Caligula and Nero, and the scabrous though riotously funny *Satyricon* of Petronius, saw also some improvements in legal protections for slaves, and the wickedness of Rome, and the treachery and madness of her political upheavals, did not mean that people living in the outlying areas were similarly treacherous and mad. As often, the country folk kept to their old ways, and as they were slow to adopt the vices of the city, so they would prove to be slow to convert to the Christian faith: hence the faintly derogatory name they were known by, *pagani*, "country bumpkins," came generally to denote adherents to the old forms of Roman religious worship.

I am delighted to grant that the stupidities of racism have largely been routed from the field. I will note, though, that we are talking here about the rejection of something rather bizarre and in important respects quite modern: for the racism of old did not call upon the sciences to blow the trumpet before it, as heralding a dawn of social progress and intelligently managed demographics. The racism of old, such as we can find it, was not racism in our modern terms at all but ethnic rivalry, Israel against Moab, Swedes against Geats, Athenians against Spartans, Greeks generally against Persians, even the Veii, a spit away from the newish city, against the first Romans, if we are to trust the ancient legends that Livy reports. I have often noted that we do not know what St. Augustine looked like, because nobody thought it worth mentioning; he was born in North Africa, his father had a Roman name, which does not prove anything, and his mother had a Punic name, which does suggest that he had Semitic blood. Did he have dark skin? Any Ethiopian mix? Red hair, like many of the Berbers? Nobody knows. A majority of the Roman emperors after the first century did not even come from Italy. Did anyone care what "race" the African, Septimius Severus, belonged to, if the Romans could even be made to understand the term as it has been used in the modern West? Legend has it that St. Thomas went to India to evangelize the Hindus. Legend does not record that anybody thought he was going among a different biological race of human persons.

Let us also cheerfully admit that most of the intellectual prejudices against women have been scouted. I do not admit that, in general, women are better treated in our time than in the past, far from it, or that they are happier, or that they and their menfolk are better people, each sex more grateful for the other than ever before. But I will admit that it is a good thing that nobody any longer thinks it odd to have a woman doctor, a woman dentist, a woman professor, and so forth.

So much we can credit to moral advance. And some more too. We are, by far, less cruel to animals than we used to be, though that judgment must be tempered; the way we raise them for food will not, I think, bear moral scrutiny. It is not that we kill them and eat them, but that we give them no real animal life at all, and in this regard the hunter who stalks and shoots deer or pheasant or grouse is much more humane, in practical action though not always in his inner intent, than is the industrialist stuffing chickens full of hormones and feed and hardly allowing them the run of an ordinary barnyard.

Our consciences are more tender regarding the treatment of children. We are apt to loathe anyone who would beat a child, though we do not scruple to kill them in the womb. Nor do we think it heinous to expose children to all kinds of moral filth in the media, or to saw their souls in half by divorce. Well, perhaps the optimist had better not look too closely into this area of moral action.

Murder rates in America — I do not know about every other country in the world — are no worse than they used to be. Whether that means we are less devoured by the wrath and hatred that lead to murder, I cannot tell. Organized crime is not as powerful as in the days of Al Capone. A much smaller percentage of our populace is in the high-violence zone: I speak of young men. The old man is not necessarily *better* than the young man, just because he is less likely to kill; he is less likely to be *able* to do it, and much less likely to be fearless about it, supposing that he were willing and able. Incapacity and timidity are not moral virtues. We must consider also our unprecedentedly antisocial way of life. Polyphemus the Cyclops is not likely to murder another of his kind, but that is not because he is good. It is because he and they have almost nothing to do with one another. People who live in self-built padded cells are not likely to kill, or to do much else that is social for good or for evil, but that has to do with their cells, not with their virtue. Show me a people who have countless dealings of all kinds, every day, with a wide variety of their fellows, and who still do not choke them or shoot them or drown them or compel them to watch *The View*, and then I will believe that they have attained a respectable degree of peacefulness and tolerance.

How can we measure a society's moral status? In my Church, the Roman Catholic, we used to be instructed, before going to

Confession, to consider the Ten Commandments one after another, in all the ways in which a person might sin against them and against the virtues they are meant to promote and to protect. We might then do the same for men and women of the current time.

First commandment: "I am the Lord thy God; thou shalt not have strange gods before me." I do not think the believer in moral progress wants to touch this one. He calls his indifference or his contempt of God a virtue. It is no hard virtue to practice. In fact, it requires you to do nothing at all. But, as I have suggested, man *will worship*, and if it is not God it will be someone or something else: wealth, sex, power, prestige, and all the other usual objects of ambition. No, I do not believe we have advanced in this regard.

Second commandment: "Thou shalt not take the name of the Lord thy God in vain." Profanity is everywhere, and obliviousness to, or scorn for, the holy. What now stops our mouths lest we offend against the sacred?

Third commandment: "Remember the Sabbath, to keep it holy." We need not think here of those grim misreadings of the commandment that sentenced people to starched suits and dead afternoons and being ill at ease. It is a commandment to feast: to see human life as oriented not toward work, ambition, money-making, or idleness, but toward joy, and that in abundance. Joy, however, cannot be manufactured. It is both a gift to the soul and the grateful overflowing of the soul in return for the gift. Consider the church bells ringing in every small parish of an Italian town. They call people together, and men are united in the depths of their beings only by some common object of devotion, so that a town without churches, so to speak, is no town at all, but a mere geopolitical fiction.

Of course, atheists will say that the fading of man's worship is a sign of progress, but we can meet them on their own terms and ask them, supposing that they do retain some measure of common humanity, what has replaced God in the hearts of men, so as to inspire them to build something as astonishing as the cathedral in Cologne, or to write something as brilliant and profoundly moving as Bach's *Passion according to St. Matthew*, or to bring people of both sexes and all ages together on a frosty night to go from house to house in their neighborhood, singing—carols, of course, but what do the faithless have to replace it with? And in the meantime, the strictly *human* benefits of the Sabbath are mostly gone. Until about ten years ago, Nova Scotia, where we live in the summer, still had laws that forbade most sorts of business on Sunday. Those laws survived one attack after another, till finally they fell—and with the predictable results. Instead of having a day when you could count on everybody being at home, Sunday has slid over into Monday, and what little casual activity you might meet in the neighborhood has faded some more. The Nova Scotians were precluded from defending the Sunday rest by saying that it helped them rightly orient their thoughts toward God and His gifts. Such an argument would get no purchase in a secular society. They refused to admit that there was a heavenly good to lose, so they ended up losing the earthly good as well.

When moral virtue *develops*, it does what the word suggests: it *unfolds*, it attains to greater power, broader application; it bears more abundant fruit; its roots penetrate more deeply into the human heart. Decay is not development. A man hobbling on a cane has not improved upon his youthful legs that once climbed trees and raced about the playing field. You do not become more honest by redefining your lies away. We revere little, and it shows: we have become slovenly and flippant, and after the first fallacious taste of the fruit of irreverence is gone, whatever laughter it provokes is mirthless and weary.

Fourth commandment: Honor thy father and mother. This is the command of *piety*, closely related to the previous command.

It is, as has been often noted, the doorway, opening in each direction, that links the commands that prescribe our duty to God to those that prescribe our duty to our fellow men. For in the family, in those most fundamental relations of husband and wife, parent and child, brothers and sisters, we learn both to worship God and to treat one another with justice and love. Jesus says that all of the law and the prophets hangs upon two commandments, which are really one: "You shall love the Lord your God with all your heart, and with all your soul, and with all your mind," and "you shall love your neighbor as yourself" (Matt. 22:36–40). In the family you will learn these things, if you learn them at all.

The commandment enjoins the children to honor and obey, and not just when they are too small to care for themselves. When my grandmother's mind was going and she could no longer feed or care for herself, my father said, in terms too blunt for me to repeat here, that if she did something for him when he was a baby, he could well do the like for her now. Honor and obedience extend for a lifetime. He never spoke ill of his own father, who drank too much and was surly when drunk; drank, to dull the constant pain of a broken neck he suffered in a mine explosion. My father liked my maternal grandfather better; but there was never any question of the duty he owed to the old man, and not once did he get in the way of our enjoying our grandfather's company.

Are grandparents a regular part of their children's children's lives? We might as well ask whether parents themselves are the leading lights in their own children's lives. When I was a boy, school devoured six or seven hours a day, five days a week, from early September to early June. It did not devour an additional hour or so every day on a bus. It did not invade August. When it was not in session, we were free. There were no summer assignments. There was not much homework anyhow. We had the considerable distractions of television, but not the computer screen and the Internet. Parents and children spent more time together, and you were likely to have aunts, uncles, and cousins near, not to mention your brothers and sisters. What man works at all, says Péguy, if not for his children? But we now reverse the relation and too often see children as hampering our more important work. Children have been relegated to a side room. If you were to design a way of life exactly calculated to keep children safe in their bodies, but to smother their souls, to stunt their imaginations, to dull their initiative, to ensure that they will be mostly lonely and sullen, to make them like aliens to the natural world surrounding them, you could not do it more precisely than we have done. So if you ask whether we have now developed, morally, in our care for children, I will respond by asking you when was the last time you saw a neighborhood swarming with children, playing games of their own devising, or by asking you how likely it is that a child will grow up with a married mother and father, or by asking you whether we do even a fair job protecting their innocence.

Fifth commandment: Thou shalt not kill. I have dealt with our static murder rates above—static, if you do not consider the million children snuffed out by abortion in the United States each year. It does not appear to me, from the history of the twentieth century, that we are less apt to slaughter countless people in war. Nor does it give me confidence in our moral advancement that we now seem to peddle death as a comfortable way out of your despair, if you decide that you are too sad to continue living. Hospitals themselves now prescribe morphine, not a new drug by any means, as a way of suppressing the respiration of people with terminal diseases, even when they are not in pain. The Hippocratic counsel to "do no harm" is ignored. In some nations, people with perfectly curable conditions will not get the care they need, because the national health services deem them to be too old. They are—but without anything like the same urgency and brute necessity—like the elderly that the people of certain nomadic tribes leave behind to die, because they can no longer make the grueling journey across the desert.

But the commandment forbids more than killing. It forbids wrath and hatred, the desire to harm, to destroy. We rightly shake our heads at men who used to duel to the death over a matter of honor. Yet those men at least had the physical courage for it. What do we make of people who from the safety of their homes set about destroying someone's career? Or of people who stoke hatreds, benefiting from it politically—a game not limited to one side of the political spectrum? Or acts of mayhem, riot, civil chaos? If you say, "Those things don't happen in our town," I will immediately ask you how much you "pay" for your relative immunity by locked doors, gated communities, security guards, and a withered social life.

Sixth commandment: Thou shalt not commit adultery. No comment. This one requires a whole book. The collapse of sexual morality has been breathtaking and disastrous. It has been what I have called the Lonely Revolution, and no longer do its adherents even bother with the pretense that it makes people happy. It has alienated them. I need not be called to witness. Their own embittered music and literature give in evidence.

Seventh commandment: Thou shalt not steal. By this commandment, we are urged to consider a man's property to be sacrosanct. It prohibits not just the more flagrant actions of burglary, highway robbery, mugging, embezzlement, and theft by invading someone's bank account. It extends to a respect for property as such, because property often is the result or the manifestation of a long human history. The land a family owns and farms is not just the soil beneath their shoes. It is the sweat of the great-grandfather who now lies in the family plot. It is the line of apple trees and peach trees that the grandfather planted in his old age, knowing that he himself would not gain much fruit by them. The house from which I am writing these words, in a room surrounded with shelves of thousands of books, is not just the wood and stone that make it up, but the countless sacrifices, investments, purchases, and acts of embellishment and repair that my wife and I have made, here and elsewhere we have lived, over the course of our entire married lives. I own books that mean more to me because I inherited them from a colleague in medieval literature, or from my friend the elderly physicist, or from priests I have known who have passed away.

Property, as Richard Weaver noted in *Ideas Have Consequences*, is about the last metaphysical object that Americans can still grasp; but that grasp has grown far more tenuous since his time. Human property — property owned by man, for man — extends far into the past and into the future. If you treat it with contempt, considering an individual's death as the opportunity to dissolve his estate and redistribute the proceeds, or levying taxes so high that intergenerational ownership becomes practically impossible, you are a kind of thief, even if your profit is political or ideological and not financial.

But property is also to be used for the common good and not just for private enjoyment, and that means that the rich have a duty to the poor. Whether this duty is discharged by a vast welfare state bristling with moral hazards that tend to keep the poor in their dependent place, I doubt very much. The *personal* duty seems not to be discharged at all. If you enjoy your million-dollar home in a neighborhood far from the sight and the smell of the poor, and you assuage your conscience by telling yourself that you vote to feed and increase that welfare state, I wonder instead whether you have not been selfish and negligent in two ways at once.

Meanwhile, under the guise of righteous indignation, many Americans in our cities wait for the next prompting to engage in what Edward Banfield, in *The Unheavenly City*, trenchantly called

"Looting Mostly for Fun and Profit," while the police look aside. Our own local post office, in a rural section of New Hampshire, taped its outdoor mailbox shut a few years ago because of the threat of "fishing" for envelopes with bank checks in them. Apparently, the problem is acute in Baltimore, and it is not limited to mere robbery. Sometimes the amount on the check is altered, so that your bank will release $5,000 instead of $50.

Theft, of course, has always been with us. Irish folk songs, as far as I can tell, have mainly to do with drinking, pretty girls, missing your homeland, beating up British soldiers, and taking somebody else's things. I have an 1883 nickel that was gold-plated by some evil-minded thief, because the coin originally did not have the word *CENTS* on it, just a V, the Roman numeral for five. The thieves would plate the nickel with gold and pass it off for five dollars. The man traveling the dangerous road between Jerusalem and Jericho fell among thieves, who robbed him, beat him, and left him for dead. And yet, when I was growing up, people left their keys in their cars all the time because it was convenient to do so. Call this one a tossup at best.

Eighth commandment: Thou shalt not bear false witness against thy neighbor. If we are to believe in progress here, we must suppose that scholars, journalists, politicians, teachers, businessmen, lawyers, and ordinary people are more scrupulously honest than ever. Scholars and scientists never exaggerate their claims; they never plagiarize; they do not smuggle desired results into the structure of their experiments to begin with; they do not claim as proof what is at best strongly suggestive; they state the opposing position in a respectful, accurate, and honest way; they do not poison the well; they do not mask political activism as even-handed and disinterested evaluation; they do not attack the careers and reputations of their opponents. Journalists try their hardest to find out exactly what happened, rather than accepting the story that comes most easily; when they report on laws, they read what they are reporting on; when they report on a scholar, they read what he has written; they do not game the system by letting one side of a controversy get the last word. Teachers do not hide their ignorance by taking the easy way out, which in our time is to discuss everything from a ready-to-hand political view; they do not hide or disguise what they are doing from the parents most concerned. And so on.

There are many ways to violate this commandment, and most of them have to do with a desire to hurt other people by destroying their reputations. Before there was such a thing as social media, you were limited in your capacity to gossip, to reveal nasty things about your neighbor, to leap to hasty conclusions at his expense and then to spread those conclusions about, and to put the worst interpretation of his words or actions. You were also restrained by a practical consideration. Your neighbor might knock on your door and ask to have a word with you. And by another practical consideration. The friends you gossip with might have a few nasty things to reveal about you, in turn, and your actions would give them the go-ahead to reveal them. People used to say that living in a small town was uncomfortable because everybody knew everybody else's business. That is true enough, but the alternative, right now, is not to live in a city where nobody knows anybody else but to stew in a worldwide cauldron of misinformation, gleeful slander, and the running down of people's good names, even driving them from their livelihoods, all without ever having to look them in the eye.

Ninth and tenth commandments: Thou shalt not covet thy neighbor's goods; thou shalt not covet thy neighbor's wife. These commandments treat of more than actions. They condemn the spiritual state that gives rise to the actions. We are not to covet: we are not to look with longing and envy on what someone else has that we do not have. I am far from the first person to note that our entire economy is fueled by covetousness, by the uneasy feeling we get when we notice that someone else has what we do not have. Imagine what would happen if we focused on meeting our real needs and moderating or restraining our desires. Imagine, that is, how many people would be able to live on a modest income, in modest homes, because their neighbors will not have, by their excesses, raised the prices of goods that all people need regardless of how poor they are, such as a place to live in, warm clothes, nourishing food, some entertainment, and means for going here and there.

I have no desire, either personal or political, to relieve any rich man of any of his property. But I also have no illusions about the moral danger of great wealth and acquisitiveness, to the person and to the society. It is not good for rich and poor to live so far apart from one another that they do not send their children to the same public schools, they do not worship at the same churches, they do not frequent the same shops, and they do not regularly meet one another on the street. The richest men in my hometown were the owner of the largest grocery store, still quite small by our standards now, the owner of the oldest pharmacy, also small by our standards, the family doctor, and the funeral director. I went to school with their children, and I played ball with them in the local Little League, as I did also with children who had to work after school to help meet the family's expenses. No one thought that was unusual.

I am not saying that laws should forbid large businesses from attempting to make inroads on the market for any particular good. It is the large trend I am noting here. It is the trend away from family-owned businesses, with all their individual characters, toward what is large, distant, impersonal, and standardized. That same hometown of mine was no energetic field of economic action. It and its neighbors had sagged into depression when the anthracite coal mines ran out; the last one to shut down, where I lived, did so when I was ten years old, though you could still get deliveries of coal to your home for the furnace. But it's quite a different way of life you enjoy, when in the normal run of a child's life he can leave the school grounds during lunch hour to grab a sandwich at the luncheonette on the main street; and when he walks home he can duck into a small pharmacy to buy a comic book; and after he changes into play clothes he goes to a family-owned grocery to pick up the newspapers he is going to deliver, while grabbing a small carton of orange juice; and when he's delivered them all, he can play baseball with the neighbor kids, because the old man who owns the yard across the street lets them use it at their pleasure.

Progress in Social Structures?

We may say that wealth has brought us great opportunity for alleviating the suffering that man, before the Industrial Revolution—and indeed during that revolution if you were so unfortunate as to work in the mills, the foundries, or the mines—took as a regular feature of his life. In 1897, the social reformer Jacob Riis described the cleansing of one of the side streets in New York City, as it had gotten choked up with mud and filth, decades of it. The firemen took their hoses and turned them on the alleys, the porches of the tenements, the culverts, and the streets nearby, sometimes causing gushers of brown mud to burst up from below. They spent all day at it, and the street was just as filthy as ever. Scoffers enjoyed their jests, but the city and the firemen did not give up, and when they returned to do a more thorough cleansing, it was as if the children in that neighborhood could breathe real air for the first time. Riis believed, with good reason, that children easily go bad, physically and morally, when they live in squalor. Hence his tireless efforts to have tenements either repaired or condemned, and his urging

American cities to clear playgrounds for children, rather than having them mainly hang around dirty alleys where bums diced for money and cigarettes and worse, and the youngsters learned to pick pockets before they learned to read.

So many are the things we take for granted! If you live in New York City now, you turn on your tap and you get fresh, clean water. If you lived there in 1860, you probably used water gathered in cisterns from rain falling on the tenement roofs, and that meant only a gallon or two per day, per household. Consider what that implies for cooking, not to mention for keeping your body clean. Tenements were firetraps too; keep in mind that you needed a fire to cook your dinner. And where did you get your food? Mostly from nearby, and that is not necessarily a bad thing, except that it also meant that many city dwellers kept chickens, and pigs went rooting for garbage in the streets.

Do you have a high fever? Forget about sulfa drugs and anti-biotics. You need to keep that fever down with ice. Where do you get it? From icehouses, and that meant, ultimately, from the huge blocks of ice that men and boys cut out of frozen lakes and ponds in the winter. But sometimes the winter was unusually warm, and the icehouses would run out of ice before the next winter came on. Then there was nothing to cool you off.

Many have been the wonders of technology, these last two hundred years: the steam engine, the combustion engine, refrigeration (the single invention most liberating to women), electric power, the automobile, the train, the airplane, the camera in all its many forms, radio, television, and now the high-speed computer, placing the world's store of knowledge and art within reach of almost everyone on earth — provided that they have the intelligence and the desire to learn. The childhood diseases that once killed or crippled so many have now been rendered mostly powerless; and a sixty-year-old man now looks younger than his grandfather did at fifty or even forty. All this is to the good, and I would be an ungrateful wretch to deny it.

But it is one thing to say that our tools are better than ever before, and quite another to say that we do better things with them. If you say that our *social structures* have evolved, I must confess that I cannot conceive of what you are talking about, since it would be like saying—I exaggerate, of course, but I wish to make the point—that our dinosaurs have evolved, because we no longer have any.

People simply do not do social things with one another as they used to, because, in part, they can get through a day without them. The loss to our lived experience is incalculable. The oldest Swedish men's choir in the United States, the Verdandi Male Chorus, one whose concerts I attended every year, and whose members I got to know as friends, because my daughter was singing in the corresponding women's choir, folded its tent in 2010 after 115 years of singing, because young men weren't interested in it. Every old church gives silent witness to choirs that are gone, sometimes in old hymnals gathering dust in a closet; and you can tell from someone's penciled notes that the books were used, and you can gauge the difficulty of what the singers did by the form of the chants or the songs. Robert Putnam called the phenomenon, in his book by that name, "bowling alone," considering as diagnostic the fading away of a really innocent form of entertainment, one that could bring together men and women, grownups and children. When I was a teenager, these things were beginning to fall away, and some of us were aware of it and took it with alarm, but the losses were gradual, and so most people shrugged and thought that it was a matter of one social activity replacing another. But it did not happen. The local rock bands that played at dance halls or firehouse halls or school gymnasiums in one small town after another in my county had their day, and they faded, and nothing replaced them. The town where I live now, according to a *Life* magazine article published in 1943, held dances every Saturday night at the town hall, and the photographs accompanying the article show a ten-year-old boy, one Jackie Hunt, dancing with a grown woman, as he always did, delighting in it. That's all gone.

The secularist who smiles to see churches boarded up, or sold off to become offices or antique stores, should keep in mind that that is happening to the buildings once owned by *all manner of social institutions*: the Elks, the Rotary Club, the small drugstore with a breakfast counter, the dance hall, the parish school, the general store, the small bowling alley, the gas station and auto repair shop, and so forth, without replacement in kind. We are rich, and our bodies are healthy, but we do so very little with our wealth and our health. Add to it the sexual revolution's confusions, treacheries, and tawdriness, and the cheapening of erotic passion, and you have what I believe is the loneliest society ever to exist on earth, an anti-society, wherein your next-door neighbor might as well live on the moon. If this is advancement, it is the advancement of morbidity, the spread of a deadly disease. It is the worst of all worlds: a collective, but no society; political allies, but no friends; sexual congress, or the paltry mockeries of it, but little of the powerful love between man and woman that used to inspire people to sing; many schools, but little education; much print, and thin literacy; politics every hour, without the polis.

THE SEVENTH LIE

Western Christian Men Are
to Blame for Everything

THERE ARE GOOD reasons why liars don't like to be recorded, but perhaps the most ironic reason, and the most satisfying to their opponents when they can catch them up, is that the lie is inherently chaotic. It unravels. For liars live so completely in the land of falsehood that they lose their grasp on reason itself, and they end up telling lies on Tuesday that contradict the lies they told on Monday. The liar wants to get away with something *in the moment*, and that means he will have a severely foreshortened view of time, no great sense of complex series of causes and effects, and a limited capacity to see the implications of his lie or of the thing he is lying in order to attain, as the lies work themselves out in logic or in time.

Shakespeare is our great dramatist of liars caught up in their own tangles. Macbeth knew very well that if he murdered the good king Duncan, his kinsman and benefactor and a guest in his home, the deed could not have an end in itself, could not be the "be-all and the end-all," and "catch, with his surcease, success," for our own bloodiness serves as a precedent to others, and thus "this even-handed justice / Commends th'ingredients of our poisoned chalice / To our own lips" (1.7.1–12). But he does the deed anyway, and must lie to cover it up, and commit more murders to silence those who do not quite believe the lie, and all the while he exhibits a more and more shockingly foolish credulity, believing the greatest liars in the play, the three witches who equivocate, "juggling fiends" as he will call them, "that palter with us in a double sense; / That keep the word of promise to our ear, / And break it to our hope" (5.7.19–22). "Sin will pluck on sin," says the Machiavellian king Richard, when events begin to spin out of his control, and he determines to murder the woman he seduced with the boldest lies in order to become his wife (*Richard III*, 4.2.63); and then he must tell a whole series of lies to his sister-in-law, the mother of a girl he desperately needs to marry in order to settle the conflict between his house of York and the enemy house of Lancaster. But when the mother proves suspicious and slow to trust him, Richard blurts out, unwittingly, the very words that condemn him:

> As I intend to prosper and repent,
> So thrive I in my dangerous affairs
> Of hostile arms! Myself myself confound!
> Heaven and fortune bar me happy hours!
> Day, yield me not thy light, nor, night, thy rest!
> Be opposite all planets of good luck
> To my proceeding if, which dear heart's love,
> Immaculate devotion, holy thoughts,
> I tender not thy beauteous princely daughter!
> (4.4.397–405)

He has spoken his own death sentence, telling a lie that will come true in a way he does not expect. In the psalmist's words, he has dug a pit and fallen into it himself. "'Tis the sport," says Hamlet, "to have the engineer / Hoist with his own petar," that is, blown up with his own bomb (*Hamlet*, 3.4.207–208). Hamlet is referring to his schoolfellows Rosencrantz and Guildenstern, who have been lying to him, acting as spies for his uncle, King Claudius. Whether the words refer also, ironically, to Hamlet, is a matter for closer study of the play.

John Milton learned from Shakespeare the way to dramatize a liar. In *Paradise Lost*, when Satan has called to council the chiefest of the devils to inquire as to what they are going to do now that they have been cast into Hell, each of four devils speaks in turn, Moloch, Belial, Mammon, and Beelzebub, with the last one playing as Satan's secret flunky, recommending as his own a plan that originated with Satan himself. What is fascinating about their speeches, full of high-flown and intelligent oratory, and not just as decoration but with all the intention of tight and unopposable reason, is that they all seem to have forgotten, by the end, the lie or lies they began with, or the concession they made to one truth, not to establish truth but to use it as the foundation for a more subtle lie. As I read it, they themselves *do not see what they have done.* Thus Moloch, who takes pride in his brute strength and prowess in warfare, begins with a great frown and bold contempt for any councils at all. While everyone else is muddling about strategy, he cries,

> shall the rest,
> Millions that stand in arms, and longing wait
> The signal to ascend, sit lingering here
> Heaven's fugitives, and for their dwelling place
> Accept this dark opprobrious den of shame,
> The prison of his tyranny who reigns
> By our delay?
> (2.54–60)

But by the time he reaches the end of his speech, he has forgotten the beginning, and reveals, unwittingly, that his true hope is that the ire of God

Will either quite consume us, and reduce
To nothing this essential, happier far
Than miserable to have eternal being:
Or if our substance be indeed divine,
And cannot cease to be, we are at worst
On this side nothing; and by proof we feel
Our power sufficient to disturb his heaven,
And with perpetual inroads to alarm,
Though inaccessible, his fatal throne,
Which if not victory is yet revenge.
(2.96–105)

Then the craven but smooth-talking Belial stands up, recognizes that Moloch has contradicted himself, calls out the contradiction, and then proceeds to fall into one of his own making. He is opposed to war because he is a coward, "timorous and slothful," says Milton (117). Belial rightly understands that God is both omnipotent and omniscient, "Not more almighty to resist our might / Than wise to frustrate all our plots and wiles" (192–193). But by the end of his speech, as he recommends sitting quietly and not stirring God up to obvious wrath, he has forgotten about that omniscience, suggesting that God might be fooled if they do nothing but harbor evil in their hearts, and "not mind us not offending" (212). The double negative is a symptom here of a mind twisted against itself. The lie bores a hole into the brain of the liar.

The phenomenon occurs in the individual but also in men bound by lies into a false society, a kind of alliance of thieves. They cannot remember what lies they told to get where they are, so they can hardly dare to trust their fellow liars, often suspecting that they will slide back into sanity and truth. And therefore must lie be heaped upon lie, and people make obeisance to one lie after another, lest the initial falsehood—which, again, they may very well have forgotten, but they yet feel as something uneasy and unreliable, like a false foundation under a suspiciously teetering edifice—be exposed. Take for example the lie of the sexual revolution, that once we discarded the old morality that governed relations between the sexes, and permitted boys and girls to "go down the long slide / like free bloody birds," to quote the poet Philip Larkin ("High Windows," 15–16), all would be well, men and women would love one another better than ever, there would be no more wars, children would be happy and well-adjusted, and harmony and understanding would spread across the world. Nobody says such nonsense now. But now other lies have had to be told to bury the first lie, such as that we have a right to do with our bodies as we please *regardless of its effects upon the common good*, and that in any case *people were just as likely to fornicate and to commit adultery in the old days as now* (which, if it were true, no revolution was needed, and Larkin was a fool to look forward to a time that had already been in his midst), and that *sexual action is constitutive of your personal being*, an individualism wholly at odds with the generally socialist dreams of the initial revolutionaries.

Progress? Did I Say Progress?

I have already scouted the silly notion that just because we have enjoyed considerable progress in our tools, we must have seen a like progress in the wisdom and the moral tenor and the creative energy of people who use the tools. It is like saying that John *must* be a better painter than Joseph is, because he gets his paints from an art store, while Joseph must get his from leaves, flowers, berries, earths, and other things he can grind in a mortar. It is like saying that the new Tappan Zee Bridge over the Hudson River *must* be more beautiful than the ancient Pont du Gard, built by the Romans as a bridge and an aqueduct over the Gardon River in France, because our pile drivers are powered by diesel fuel and theirs were merely mechanical. It is like saying that I have an advantage over Virgil in writing poetry, because I have a word processor and he had to rely on papyrus and ink, or clay tablets and a stylus.

But if you do place great stock in technological progress—the main arena, by far, of progress in the modern world—then it seems downright madness to despise the principal authors of that progress, and to blame it for destroying the primitive forms of life that men lived, who did not have our engines, our fuel, our methods of growing and storing nourishing food, our methods of making our discoveries permanent, our means of spreading information among billions, and so on. As my own attitude toward modernity is at best ambivalent, I have cause to lament the homogenization of human cultures as our tools are brought into every once-isolated hamlet and hollow in the world. But that lament is largely forbidden to the believer in progress.

You cannot have both things at once. If in fact you believe, for example, that the way of life the Sioux lived was superior, was to be preserved at all costs, before the railroads and the telegraphs and the modernizing farmers and ranchers came, then you must cast a cold eye on the railroads, telegraphs, and tractors. If you will admit, grudgingly, that people must have food after all, and you will allow those machines to do their work, you must cast a cold eye on the agricultural developments that have replaced the family farm with vast stretches of industry-farmed fields of soybeans and such. In either case, you must give up your progressivism, if by that you imply that greater sophistication in technology must always result in greater human welfare—in other words, if you hold a lazy belief in "evolution" as an irresistible force always leading onwards and upwards. If the men were villains, you can be no progressive, because they brought the progress; but if you are a progressive, you cannot be sentimental and romantic about the Sioux, calling the men villains for bringing them the progress you believe in. I am not talking about individuals here, who in any large social movement may be good or evil, nor am I even talking about the behavior of the American government in general toward the Indians, a behavior commonly marked by treachery and callousness toward their welfare. I am talking about the large transformation of technologically primitive cultures by means of technological progress.

In this regard, the ingratitude and self-contradictions of feminists appear quite astonishing. For a hundred years, from one invention to another—the sewing machine, the refrigerator, the vacuum cleaner, the modern oven, the washing machine, the dryer, and the dishwasher—inventors (almost all of them male) have obviated almost all the difficult physical labor that women used to do. No more the drudgery of grinding some corn in a quern; no more gathering firewood; no more the exacting labor of preserving fruits and vegetables for consumption through the winter months; no more wringing clothes by hand or in a mangle; no more hanging clothes out to dry, then to be ironed flat by the pressure of your arm and the weight of the iron. Of course, much of the physical labor that men used to do has also been cleared out of the way—but by no means so thoroughly, and the tools that men use often require just as much strength and sweat as the former tools did but are more efficient in their action. So a man with a jackhammer is being taxed to the limit, to hold the thing steady while it fairly rattles his bones apart. He is doing more work than he would do with a pick and a shovel, but the work itself is just as hard; and even at that, there is still a lot he must do with that pick and shovel. A big chain saw is more efficient than a handsaw, but it is far more dangerous, and it requires much the same strength to use against tree trunks. What I mean here is that men's inventions for use around the house have profited women far more than they have profited men, and thus have set women at far greater liberty than they have set men; and yet feminists give the men no credit for it at all.

Let us come to cases. What set the middle-class woman in Victorian England, in America, in France, in Germany, free to develop talents in music and art, and to try her hand, as countless women did, at poetry and the writing of romances? The labor saved by technological progress. Now, imagine that you are a woman living in the arid reaches of southern and peninsular California, in the days before the priests arrived to teach the natives the arts of agriculture, to bring them the vine and the olive, to set about breeding many thousands of cattle and sheep. No more gathering roots and berries; no more trudging among the lizards and rattlesnakes; no more fear, even, from hostile and more warlike tribes, because the Mexican army has outposts, and they protect the missions.

You do not have to scrounge for food. Your people are the richest in America, north of the Rio Grande and west of the Mississippi. You will be despoiled of your wealth in the aftermath of the Mexican War, and the missions will be destroyed. But for the years when the fathers were here, as one old woman told Helen Hunt Jackson, who documented the history of the missions and interviewed the survivors she could find many decades later, life was good, and food was plentiful, and the arts flourished. For it was not the Europeans mainly who built the churches and painted them, and the women wove bright clothing for themselves and their men and their children, with looms that the fathers brought; and they could bring their corn to the mill to be ground, so that they had bread all the time. In a few decades, a small number of Franciscan friars did for the Indians what all the northern American progressives did not do or would not do with the freed slaves, making them into "masons, carpenters, plasterers, soap-makers, tanners, shoe-makers, blacksmiths, millers, bakers, cooks, brick-makers, carters and cart-makers, weavers and spinners, saddlers, ship hands, agriculturalists, herdsmen, vintagers;—in a word, they filled all the laborious occupations known to civilized society" (from the special report of the Honorable B. D. Wilson to the Interior Department, 1852; cited by "H. H." in "Father Junipero and His Work, II," *The Century Magazine*, June 1883: 205). The friars kept scrupulous and thorough records, so we know how many head of sheep and cattle a single mission would have, and the hundreds of thousands of acres they would have devoted to grazing and farming. Jackson again:

> The picture of life in one of these missions during their period of prosperity is unique and attractive. The whole place was a hive of industry: trades plying indoors and out-doors; tillers, herders, vintagers by hundreds, going to and fro; children in schools; women spinning; bands of young men practicing on musical instruments; music, the scores of which, in many instances, they had themselves written out; at evening, all sorts of games of running, leaping, danc-ing, and ball-throwing, and the picturesque ceremonies of a religion which has always been wise in availing herself of beautiful agencies in color, form, and harmony. (205)

All that would be ruined by the lead-up to and the prosecution and aftermath of the Mexican War, and these same mission Indians would be reduced to landlessness and bitter poverty. "I have seen the poorest huts of the most poverty-stricken wilds in Italy, Bavaria, Norway, and New Mexico, but never have I seen anything, in shape or shelter for human creatures, so loathsome as the kennels in which some of the San Diego Indians are living" ("The Present Condi-tion of the Mission Indians in Southern California," *The Century Magazine*, August 1883: 522).

Jackson witnessed it firsthand, reviewed the records, and spoke with the elderly who remembered the bright specifics of their old way of life. While Americans were trumpeting their progress west, they would not come near, not for a long time, what the friars had done in a worldly sense, and as for the spiritual life, they would never attain such a height, nor does it appear that they—we—ever shall, not unless we are the beneficiaries of a miracle of God.

Now, then, does the feminist wish to denounce the testimony of one of the bravest and most thoroughgoing women authors of her time, and in her cause, too, to champion the rights of the dispossessed Indians? But to acknowledge that Jackson was a truth teller in describing the lives of the mission Indians before the intrusion of government meddling and wartime taxation from Mexico, and violence and treaty breaking from the rest of America, they must grant that the friars knew what they were doing, and that the technological innovations they brought did profit the Indians immensely. You cannot have things both ways. You cannot say that women are especially vulnerable to poverty, *and then deny to men the credit for having lifted their societies out of that poverty.* Would the feminists really prefer that the Indian women had *not* been made the beneficiaries of the tools and the machines that European men had invented, and that their own men learned to build, to repair, and to operate? Or, to put it in a different way: the only environment in which feminism can even begin to poke its head from out of the bushes is one in which women are as safe in their persons as they can ever be, and they need do no difficult physical labor, and food is readily available in all seasons. But that world was made by men, and in the form that prevails across the world, we are mainly talking about the men of the West.

Religion? Was I Talking about Religion?

In the West, now, when people say they have no use for "organized religion," they really intend some kind of snobbish pride, or some sexual licentiousness. They mean that they do not care to associate with Christians, they do not want to attend church services, and they want to confirm some irregularity or immorality in their sexual behavior. They will use the phrase "organized religion" as a way of excusing themselves from having to oppose *all religious belief*, because then they might look like bigots, and besides, a nagging little voice in the conscience whispers to them that they should not burn all the bridges behind them as they proceed along in unbelief. Of course, religion by its very nature *must be organized*, just as all human enterprises are, because otherwise all we are talking about is a feeling in your gut, or a quirky little habit you keep to yourself, a private vice, or something of no importance at all. People who love God want to worship Him together, as fully human beings; and if you honor God as the Creator of all things, including the human race, it is a contradiction in terms to suppose that your worship of Him should be skulking, craven, and merely a matter of individual taste. No man sings to himself alone, not really, because even if he is singing to himself, he still sings with his fellows in his memory or his imagination. "I was glad when they said to me," says the psalmist, "'Let us go to the house of the LORD,'" a house of prayer and worship and song (Ps. 122:1). "Where two or three are gathered in my name," says Jesus, "there am I in the midst of them" (Matt. 18:20), and though Jesus says we should never playact at prayer in order to be gawked at by other people, He taught people by the thousands, He prayed with His disciples, He instituted the Blessed Sacrament with His prayer at the Last Supper, and the first Christians gathered together to remember His words and His deeds and to pray together and to sing, as St. Paul puts it, "psalms and hymns and spiritual songs" (Eph. 5:19).

What then is supposed to be the problem with "organized" religion? You will hear the reply that such religion—especially the monotheistic faiths—is inherently divisive and warlike. Islam, in its history, has been warlike, no question of that. *But man himself is warlike*: he has never needed religious faith to pitch him into battle, and in fact, with the partial exception of Islamic wars, almost every war in human history has had nothing to do with religion. I am weary of having to repeat this, but the historical record is abundantly clear. The Romans shut the door of the temple of Janus whenever the state was at peace; that door remained open constantly, for centuries, until finally Augustus Caesar, who styled himself the Prince of Peace, shut it. Temporarily, that is—for Rome was almost never at peace afterwards, either. The noblest of the Roman emperors, Marcus Aurelius, disliked war, but he was almost constantly away from the city, fighting against Germanic invaders pressing the frontiers of the empire, or putting down uprisings among conquered peoples within.

It is the same wherever you go. The Greek city-states were constantly quarreling, often breaking out into war, including the disastrous great conflict between Athens and Sparta, drawing into war almost all the other states, till it ended with Athenian democracy shattered, and the democrats of Athens eager to blame the aristocrats, the generals, even Socrates, whom they sentenced to death; anybody but themselves. The poet of *Beowulf* describes a way of life built upon killing people, even your own kin, and taking their wealth, breeding resentment among the defeated, and blood feuds that seemed to go on until one side was quite obliterated. The good man Beowulf himself, the best sort of pagan that the Christian poet can imagine, says that the Danish king Hrothgar was attempting to make peace with his longtime enemies by means of a marriage union. But at the marriage feast itself, says the wise young warrior, an old man, desirous of causing trouble, will whisper to some lad, and cause him to notice the sword dangling at the side of one of the enemies, a sword that belonged to the lad's father in the old days. And thus will the suggestion of vengeance come, and the swaggerer be found dead, and war will resume.

Men have fought for vengeance, bloodlust, wealth, land, and glory. They have been motivated by wrath, fear, pride, even boredom. Americans have not had more than forty years of uninterrupted peace, and we pride ourselves on being a pacific people. What needs explaining is not war, which we find everywhere we find man, but something other than war. What needs explaining is not the exploitation of the poor, but care for their welfare. What needs explaining is not the whorehouse, the gambling den, the dueling field, the sick man dying in a ditch, the abandoned wife, the poor man starving, the child sold into slavery or made into a sexual plaything, the crippled baby smothered or exposed in the wilds; these things are endemic to mankind. What needs explaining is what the Christian faith has brought—and here, meaning no disrespect, I suggest also that it is what Jews have brought too, where they have gone.

What is that? Even through the fog and confusion and self-deception that beset human motives, we can detect a distinction between what some Christians, at some times, have done in warfare and what everyone else has done. Take the case most frequently thrown in the face of Christians—the Crusades. I will not justify every battle and every warrior, and certainly the sack of Constantinople in 1204 was a disaster for the very same Byzantine Empire that the Crusaders were initially, and by the emperor himself in 1096, called on to defend from the aggressions of the Seljuk Turks. Islam had, in fact, spread like wildfire across the southern Mediterranean and the Near East, and Christian victories against Islamic invasions were mainly defensive, as by Charles Martel at Tours in 732, and by the emperor Leo the Isaurian in 717–718, when, assisted by a naphthalene concoction called "Greek fire," he raised a yearlong Muslim siege against Constantinople. For more than three hundred years, then, Christians could go on pilgrimages to the Holy Land unmolested, regardless of who was in control of the area, but then the Turks came, overcoming their fellow Muslim rulers, pressing hard against the Greeks, and making pilgrimages impossible. So when Urban VII at Clermont called for a war to assist the Greeks and liberate the Holy Land, Christian rulers and knights responded with a deeply religious enthusiasm that we now find hard to understand. If we say that they fought for land, the answer is that the rulers had land aplenty where they were, and when they left for the Holy Land, they had no assurance, even if they did return, that they could simply resume their positions of power as before. If we say that they fought for wealth, the answer is that most of them did not grow wealthy at all, and some of them impoverished themselves in order to fight. If we say that they fought to establish colonies, the answer is that they had absolutely no notion of what we mean by that word; and the Crusader kingdoms in the East were independent of European rule, as centralization and the modern state had not yet occurred. They believed they were fighting to set a land and a people free—the oppressed Christians who had long been living in those places; and, at their best, they believed they were dying as martyrs for Christ.

"Greater love has no man than this," says Jesus, "that a man lay down his life for his friends" (John 15:13). That is the key. I hold no brief for the American Civil War, and many of its political causes are embarrassing to one side or the other, to the expansionist and avaricious North, to the slave-holding and slavery-extending South. But it is certainly true that many men from the North were motivated by the reverse of self-interest: the white Robert Gould Shaw, for example, led the first all-Negro company of soldiers to battle in South Carolina, where they fought heroically and where Shaw died a hero's death. Shaw, at least, was fighting *for the sake of other people to whom he was not kin, and from whom he could expect no material or political advantage*, and not as a mercenary but as a freely self-giving soldier. Why did American boys storm the beaches of Normandy? Hitler posed no threat to the United States. They did so—or many of them did so—because it was the right thing to do, to set the beleaguered people of Western Europe free from his madness and dictatorial aims. Consider as a diagnostic case the fictional Rick, in the film *Casablanca*, who runs Rick's American Café, keeping out of politics, cynically indifferent to the forces of resistance against the Nazis, even though his own headwaiter is a member of the resistance, as he well knows. Rick's moral reclamation as a man follows a fundamentally Christian script: repentance, forgiveness, and self-sacrifice, giving up the love of his life, because it is the right thing to do, and abandoning his livelihood and all his material goods. He will fight again.

I am not saying that the crusading motivation justifies your desire to fight. Even if your motive is right, it may be foolish or downright wicked to go to war, if for example you have no fair hope for success, or you are likely to make matters worse by fighting than by sitting still or by less flagrant means than bloodshed. And then perhaps your end is mistaken. The Crusaders were aware that their fighting was as a form of penance for their sins, and that they must pay for deeds of wickedness performed in war as without. Now suppose that you still have the crusading spirit but it has been detached from Christian discipline, which compels you to remember that your deeds must be judged by the all-wise God, who cannot be fooled by slogans or war songs, and who will not bless any means you employ to compass your end. Then all bets are off. Woodrow Wilson had a strain of crusading puritanism in him that helped to pitch the United States into a monstrously bloody and purposeless war, to "make the world safe for democracy," as he said. We see what was going on. The transcendent aims of the Christian faith, which assures us or warns us, depending on how you view it or what your political ambitions are, that we have no settled kingdom here on earth, have been transposed to the worldly and political sphere. The Crusaders fought for the earthly Jerusalem as a place of pilgrimage for Christians who were on the road toward the heavenly Jerusalem. The earthly Jerusalem for its own sake was not the object. But the object of all secular progressivism, unmoored from the aims, the direction, the restrictions, the consolations, and the warnings of the Christian faith is an earthly Jerusalem—what Malcolm Muggeridge trenchantly called "the kingdom of heaven on earth," which otherwise goes by the name of Hell.

Hence the astonishingly destructive fury of the secular progressive in action, regardless of whatever may be his personal characteristics. You see it in the set jaw of the international teenage scold, Greta Thunberg, who shows not the slightest consideration for peoples in the still-developing world who require and will for the foreseeable future require the use of fossil fuels. You see it in the blithe careless-ness with which politicized climate alarmists would consign billions of human beings to death. You see it in the maddened rage of femi-nists marching for the right to kill the unborn children whose very existence is owing to the voluntary actions of the children's parents. Such fury builds nothing, but it is remarkably efficient in cultural destruction. Think of a secular John Calvin, unbound from any fears that he might be sentenced to eternal damnation, identifying a new Original Sin—patriarchy, industrialism, modern agriculture, even religious faith itself—and setting himself the holy task, like a new John Brown, of rooting it out by political force. What difference did it make to Stalin if an old and solid farming culture in the Ukraine was obliterated? You have to break some eggs to make an omelet, as his murderous predecessor Lenin said. What difference does it make to the secular crusader if a man is exposed to hatred for expressing the wrong political beliefs and loses his livelihood? Grind the resisters to powder, and mortar with their remains the bricks of the new city.

Corruptio optimi pessima est: the better a thing is, the worse it becomes when it is corrupted. C. S. Lewis put it well:

> The better stuff a creature is made of — the cleverer and stronger and freer it is — then the better it will be if it goes right, but also the worse it will be if it goes wrong. A cow cannot be very good or very bad; a dog can be both better and worse; a child better and worse still; an ordinary man, still more so; a man of genius, still more so; a superhuman spirit best — or worst — of all. (*Mere Christianity*, "The Shocking Alternative," 53).

In his apocalyptic novel *That Hideous Strength*, he shows what happens to a Christian faith without Christ, and thus without love, without the fear of God, without humility — without restraint: all-ambitious and ever looking toward the future for the consummation of human history. "Don't you see," says the former priest Straik to the muddle-headed progressive sociologist Studdock, as they discuss the new man to be manufactured by man, and to control all men and make them one, "that we are offering you the unspeakable glory of being present at the creation of God Almighty? Here, in this house, you shall meet the first sketch of the real God. It is a man — or a being made by man — who will finally ascend the throne of the universe. And rule forever" ("Moonlight at Belbury," 179). And Straik is under no illusions that this progressive leap can be made without violence and bloodshed.

Do you think it is bad to live among people who believe that God, who is love, demands that they love Him with all their heart and soul and mind and strength, and that they love their neighbors as themselves? Wait until you find the same fervor devoted to political action, whose fuels are wrath, ambition, hatred, vengeance, and envy.

Living among Human Beings

What the Christian—and, yes, Jewish—West has brought to mankind is the notion of universality, whose groundwork had been laid likewise by the greatest of the pagan Greek and Roman philosophers, statesmen, and poets.

There is a chilling episode of the old television crime show *Hawaii Five-0*, in which a family of rubes from the Midwest go on a spree of killing and petty thievery. When they are finally caught, their matriarch calmly defends their actions. They did not steal anything, she says, because the people they were supposed to have stolen from were already dead. And they did not murder those people, because, she says, "They weren't kin." It doesn't count as killing if your victims are not your kin.

Nobody can believe such a thing? On the contrary, that is the default position for man, bloody and treacherous man, marred by Original Sin. Go among Aboriginal tribes and learn their languages, and you will often find that they call themselves by the general appellation of "people" or "human beings," suggesting that those who are outside of their kin group do not merit the title, and thus do not warrant any protection or respect, unless they are bound to you by some act of alliance, easy to break. Why did the Iroquois fight the Delaware and reduce them to misery, calling them "women"? Because it was glorious to do so. Was it wrong for them to do that? They would have laughed at the suggestion. How could it be wrong? The Delaware were their enemies, and that was that. Not kin: not human.

When, in *Le Chanson de Roland* (*The Song of Roland*), the great Christian warrior Roland, defending the pass at Roncesvalles against the ambush of the Muslim enemy, says, "*Paien unt tort et Chrestien unt dreit,*" "Pagans are in the wrong and Christians are in the right" (1015), he is not speaking of race or kinship but of an entire orientation toward God. If we feel our flesh prickle at the saying, we should keep in mind that Roland's view is a vast improvement over what man usually thinks and does, not to mention the question of whether Roland is in this regard simply correct. Either Christ is the coeternal Son of God, as Christians believe, or He is not, as Muslims believe, regardless of the honor they grant to Him as a prophet lesser than Mohammed. If He is, then it behooves man to know it and to follow Him. In fact, the one consideration that Roland's king Charlemagne is prone to, that he must consider regardless of the danger to his kingdom and his person, is that the Saracen king Marsilion has promised to convert to the Christian faith. That is the key that the traitor Ganelon will play upon, setting the stage for the disastrous ambush. Says Charlemagne, deep in thought, when his ambassador Blancandrin reports what Marsilion has promised: "*Uncore purrat guarir*," "He may yet be made whole" (156). Notice the emperor's emphasis. It is not "We may twist his arm so that he becomes one of us." It is not "We may win him over so that we no longer have to worry about him." It is rather "He may yet be made whole" — that is, he still has a chance to be healed. *That* is the new thing to be explained: the care for the enemy. It is in accord with the teaching of Jesus, that we are to pray for our enemies, and do good to those who do evil to us, so that we may be true children of our Father in Heaven, who makes His rain to fall upon both the just and the unjust (cf. Matt. 5:38–48).

We see that universality set forward in the Old Testament. Consider: the Roman slave never had a day off. Why should he? The Romans were brilliant and innovative engineers, but the cheap and ready availability of slave labor meant that they never had cause to turn their minds toward agricultural improvements. Slavery stalls a society's technological development, just as water flows downhill, and people in general take the path of least immediate resistance. But among the Jews it was not to be so, for "the seventh day is a sabbath to the LORD your God; in it you shall not do any work, you, or your son, or your daughter, your manservant, or your maidservant, or your cattle, or the sojourner who is within your gates" (Exod. 20:10). The stranger is to be treated well, for we are all wayfarers in this world, and the children of Israel themselves were strangers in Egypt: "When a stranger sojourns with you in your land, you shall not do him wrong. The stranger who sojourns with you shall be to you as the native among you, and you shall love him as yourself; for you were strangers in the land of Egypt: I am the LORD your God" (Lev. 19:33–34). Thus when King David took to himself the wife of his faithful soldier Uriah the Hittite, and then connived to have the innocent man die in battle, God punished him most severely. For Uriah, a worshipper of God though he was not ethnically Jewish or even Semitic (the Hittites were Indo-Europeans, and their language is a distant cousin of English), was a Hittite and thus a stranger in the land, and that *exacerbated David's crime and compounded his guilt* (cf. 2 Sam. 11).

The God whose name is beyond names, suggesting the act of Being itself, is not bound to an ethnic group or to a political system, or to any place and time. He has chosen Israel; but the prophets remind the people that He has done so not because they are especially good. The reverse is true: because God has chosen them, they are enjoined to be holy. For the rule of God extends to all people: "A multitude of camels shall cover you, the young camels of Midian and Ephah; all those from Sheba shall come. They shall bring gold and frankincense, and shall proclaim the praise of the LORD" (Isa. 60:6). The universality is confirmed and extended to the uttermost by Christ Himself, who sends forth His disciples with the command to "make disciples of all nations, baptizing them in the name of the Father and of the Son and of the Holy Spirit" (Matt. 28:19), who found in the Roman centurion a faith greater than He found in all of Israel (cf. Matt. 8:10), and who sent Paul as a "chosen instrument," to bear His name "before the Gentiles and kings and the sons of Israel" (Acts 9:15), and Paul did that very thing, preaching that in Christ there is neither Greek nor Jew, neither free man nor slave. "In Christ there is no east or west," says the American hymn,

> In him no south or north,
> But one great fellowship divine
> Throughout the whole wide earth.

Now there are two fundamental ways to conceive of human universality. One is to smother all important differences among people, to obliterate nations, cities, churches, schools, and families insofar as these retain any deeply distinguishing characteristics, so that you end up with thousands of shades of gray. The other is to affirm those characteristics while cleansing them of wickedness and stupidity, so that as they grow holier, they grow more distinctly themselves, not less, *and thus the readier to unite in genuine fellowship with others.* Thomas Aquinas says that, since angels are not individuated by matter, each one of them is as it were his own species (*Summa Theologiae* I., q. 50, art. 4); and yet the angels are in fundamental and unbreakable union with one another, and their characteristic corporate actions in Scripture suggest harmony: they fight in ranks, and they worship in ranks. They are the hosts, that is, the armies of Heaven. I bring the point up not because I claim any special knowledge of the study of angels but to suggest an analogy. We human beings in our distinct nations and families, our cultures and languages, stand between the beasts and the angels. Dogs form packs, but one pack is much the same as another. There is no history to the pack, nothing in the moment that transcends, in the consciousness and the willed actions of the dogs, the time in which they live.

They are drawn along by the river of time, inevitably and naturally, while human beings not only resist the river by creating things that outlast them; they stand above and beside the river in their thought, in the essential orientation of their souls. Nation, family, culture, language—human language, that is, invented by human beings and capable, even among cultures that have no writing, to elevate the individual beyond himself and his place and time—are not to be dismissed as arbitrary or meaningless. I am suggesting *that it is a good thing that there are distinct nations, families, cultures, and languages*, because without them man would be the less, would be no more than an aggregate of disconnected individuals with nothing between them and a vast, impersonal collective, something that arouses no love and that can claim no legitimate allegiance. It is to turn all men out of their homes.

It is said that Christian missionaries do in fact turn the pagans out and render them without a cultural home. But two millennia of experience suggest that that is not so. The paradigmatic approach is to be found in the letters of Pope Gregory the Great to the missionary Augustine of Canterbury. The question was whether the Christians should tear down the pagan temples. Gregory said no, they should not. They should cleanse them and rededicate them to the worship of Christ, and they may continue to kill beasts in the vicinity, not to offer them as sacrifices to demons but for a feast, in praise of God who has given them the good things of the earth to enjoy (cf. Bede, *Ecclesiastical History of the English People*, 1.30; the letter was written in 601, to Abbot Mellitus, who was to report to Augustine). We find it no surprise, then, that when the people of England become Christian, their expression of that faith is markedly Germanic. They were not to dress like Romans, speak like Romans, sing like Romans, and so forth. The same author who preserves for us the letters I have mentioned, Bede the Venerable, also records for us the story of the cattle keeper Caedmon, an illiterate man who, one night, left the beer feast that his fellow workers were celebrating in one of the outbuildings beside the monastery of Stranaeshalch (4.24). The old Germanic war songs were going round the table along with the harp, and Caedmon, who did not know any songs—or who, perhaps, did not want to sing what songs he knew—got up to tend the cattle before retiring for the night. When he fell asleep, an angel of the Lord appeared to him in a dream and commanded him to sing something.

"I don't know anything to sing," said Caedmon, but the angel was insistent, and Caedmon asked him what he should sing.

"*Sing me frumsceaft*," said the angel, in the Anglo-Saxon tongue. "Sing me the first-shaping."

And at that, Caedmon sang a hymn of creation, not in Roman verse, not in Roman form, but in the centuries-old alliterative form of Germanic poetry, using words and images that were characteristic of that poetry, and giving them a new meaning. The combination is stunning, and it set the stage for English Christian poetry for the next three hundred years. How powerful it is to read, in the remarkable and thoroughly Germanic *The Dream of the Rood*, of Christ striding toward Calvary like a warrior:

> *Ongyrede hine tha geong Haeleth—*
> > *thaet waes God aelmihtig,*
> *strang ond stithmod;*
> > *gestah he on gealgan heanne,*
> *modig on manigra gesyhthe,*
> > *tha he wolde mancyn lysan.*

> Then the young hero ungirt himself,
> > that was God almighty,

strong and stiff-willed,
    and strode to the horrible gallows,
mood-firm in the sight of many;
    intended to set mankind free.
(39–41)

Should we expect the same poetic sense, the same way of looking at things, in China as among the formerly pagan Angles? Of course not. Mass marketing may teach Vietnamese people to sing "Jingle Bells." There is something appalling about that. But not when a people make the Faith their own, or perhaps I should say that the Faith makes them more purely themselves than they were before.

Again I turn to Lewis, and a passage in *That Hideous Strength* that bears upon both universality and the goodness of distinctions:

> If one is thinking simply of goodness in the abstract, one soon reaches the fatal idea of something standardized — some common kind of life to which all nations ought to progress. Of course, there are universal rules to which all goodness must conform. But that's only the grammar of virtue. It's not there that the sap is. He doesn't make two blades of grass the same: how much less two saints, two nations, two angels. The whole work of healing [Earth] depends on nursing that little spark, on incarnating that ghost, which is still alive in every real people, and different in each. When Logres really dominates Britain, when the goddess Reason, the divine clearness, is really enthroned in France, when the order of Heaven is really followed in China — why, then it will be spring. ("Venus at St. Anne's," 4)

The progressive is imperialist and colonialist by necessity, almost by definition. Behind the marquee of human rights, for example, he would destroy every culture on earth, because the single *earthly* thing that most characterizes a culture and distinguishes it from its neighbors is how the people get the boys and girls married, to bring children into being and to raise them well. But if all of that must be shunted into the vast international sewage river of sexual confusion, all to be justified by feminism and the promotion of homosexual behavior, then in this central regard there may as well be no nations at all and no peoples, as there will also be no cultures, properly speaking. We may say analogous things about political structures and electoral machinery. Why, President Wilson, must the world be made safe for democracy? Why should it not harbor monarchy too, and aristocracy, or whatever characters or combinations of social structures a people find most amenable to their way of life? But there spoke the gaunt and pale scholar, whose soul was inhabited by a single and all-dissolving idea.

The Christian faith, I affirm, is for all men as individual saints and as nations sweetly and sharply distinct from one another. Progressivism is to this faith as the dreary and place-scorning international style in architecture is to a good old English home tucked into a hillside; as megalomania is to true greatness of heart; as a shopping mall stocked with mass-produced garbage is to a gift made by hand and laid beneath the tree; as a standardized curriculum mass-marketed to millions of children in a once-free nation is to a couple of friends talking about a book they both love; as an abstract and bloodless definition of love is to the frolic gamesomeness of a family well-pleased with one another, alike in their hair and eyes and noses and dizzyingly unlike in their personalities. You say you want diversity? A single family that has somehow escaped the standardizing and progressive forces of mass schooling and mass entertainment will give you more than enough to handle.

THE EIGHTH LIE

Statistics

MANY OF THE lies that batter our minds are hard to group according to their objects, but easier to group according to their means. Mark Twain famously said that there were "lies, damned lies, and statistics." His general point can be grasped if we include under the category of "statistics" all those lies that gather acceptance from being repeated ad nauseam, with the approval of supposed authorities in whatever field we are talking about. In other words, it is not only the shifty use of mathematics that spreads falsehood. It is also the shifty use of ostensibly scientific categories and analysis. Almost always, those who engage in such falsehood, whether they are aware of it as falsehood or not (and often enough they are not, for stupidity and folly do much of the necessary work, while cunning and wickedness lie in their hammocks and muse about worse things to visit upon mankind born to die), do so for a political or economic cause. The motive, good or bad, does not in itself make the means good or bad, or true or false, but when power and money are in play, do not expect mankind to be very careful at reasoning. And since most people are somewhat in awe of numbers, or of terms got up in the garb of science, they are the likelier to fall prone before falsehood in such forms, and to spread it, and to make it almost impossible to dislodge it from their minds.

Let us take these falsehoods in a few characteristic forms.

Insidious Combination of Like with Unlike
Or we may call this a refusal to disambiguate.

Who is the safest person in the United States? A married woman, married only once, living with her husband. She is least likely to be the victim of a felony crime. She is least exposed to the dangers of the world roundabout. The home, even if she spends much of the day outside of it, is a haven for her. Look at things with the eye of a criminal, a bad or violent man. You pass by a well-tended home with a garden outside and the signs of children's play, and it enters your consciousness that a grown man may be behind that door, one who is absolutely committed to the welfare of his wife and children. He might have a gun. Who knows what you will have to reckon with? You pass that house by.

Or we may look at the matter from the other direction, that is, we may ask what kinds of people *may be invited into that home*. It stands to reason that neither the husband nor the wife is going to welcome a bad man, or, without some bond of kinship, close friendship, or business partnership, any man at all, and never any man who is not a brother or a cousin unless the husband is at home. But the woman living alone will, in the preponderant majority of cases, be inviting men to come and visit, and every one of those men will be like a card you draw face down from the pack, and you do not know what you will get. Most of them will not do the woman any harm. Most—not all.

For the single woman dealing with a single man, outside of the protection of her father and her brothers, the addition of sexual attraction or sexual hunger is like scattering gasoline and gunpowder here and there across the flat. And if you consider, further, our taking for granted that people will have sexual intercourse before marriage, before love, even sometimes before acquaintance, and if you consider also that people in such circumstances only rarely agree in how important they believe the relationship to be, or if there is any relationship at all, and then if you add the factors of insecurity, disappointment, jealousy, disaffection, hurt feelings, anger, and vindictiveness, the wonder is not that these situations often set the stage for violence but that the violence is no worse than it is.

Such being the case, you would think that feminists who have the welfare of women in mind would urge them to marry and to stay married. They do not. They do the reverse. A friend of mine says that a feminist is a woman who hates men almost as much as she hates other women — especially women who are comfortable around men. Thus was born the category of "domestic violence," a category that cries out for disambiguation. We slander husbands badly by lumping them in with live-in boyfriends, or with men that take up residence sporadically. These categories of men are starkly different, and the men behave in starkly different ways. Yes, it is true that some husbands beat their wives. We are talking about probabilities, not bare possibilities. Suppose your mortal enemy gives you a choice. You can play Russian roulette with a revolver containing six chambers and one bullet, or you can play it with a special revolver he has made containing one hundred chambers and one bullet. Which one are you going to choose?

We can add, too, that since insecurity will always tempt human beings to behave erratically, and all the more so if they believe they have little that is certain to put at risk, *all of the bad things short of violence that men and women do to one another are more likely in the unstable situation than in the stable one.* Marriage is good for both sexes; shacking up, long delays in marriage, bed-hopping, fornication, and sex between near-strangers are bad for both sexes. Since women are far more vulnerable physically than men, everything that is bad puts them at a greater risk of physical harm.

Separate the categories. A (first and only) husband is a woman's best protection; the live-in boyfriend is a great danger; a young woman living alone is vulnerable in ways that the married woman can hardly imagine.

Learn about Conditional Probability

I have heard, for decades now, that most cases of child molestation involve heterosexual men, and that therefore we should not be suspicious if the gay man across the street invites your teenage son to come over to his attic to check out his big train set, or something.

First, we have the problem above, the refusal to disambiguate. You are a married man, and you want to know who is a threat to your son or your daughter. You are thinking of people outside the home. You know quite well that *you are no threat*, because you know your own behavior. You are not thinking about incest. You have no need to think about it. I do not mean to make light of that heinous evil. But it is ineradicable, unless we are going to stop having children at all. I will suggest, later, what can make it and other evils far less likely. For now, I note that the inclusion of incest in the category of child molestation is politically motivated: it is meant to obscure where the greater threat lies.

And here we must try to get into the habit of asking questions about conditional probability. Most criminals are right-handed, by far. What does that mean? By itself, it means nothing since *most people* are right-handed. We do not want to know how likely it is that a criminal will be right-handed, but rather, given a right-handed person, how likely it is that he will be a criminal. We place the condition where it belongs. We do not want to know, in the United States, how likely it is that a criminal will belong to this or that race or ethnic group, but, given a person of this or that race or ethnic group, how likely it is that he will be a criminal. Getting the condition correct is a matter of logic, but it is quite urgent when the condition makes all the difference in the world.

Let us consider, for the sake of simplicity, that we are talking about males who molest children, and leave the female molesters out of it. Since heterosexual males outnumber homosexual males by an enormous margin—between 20 to 1 and 40 to 1, depending upon what definition you use—we should expect that boys would be molested only rarely. Even if some of the boys are molested by apparently heterosexual men acting out an evil and repressed fantasy, we are still talking about what would be a small minority of the children who are victims. But that is not the case. Boys are molested by someone outside of the home about as often as girls are; perhaps half as often, perhaps just as often, and perhaps a little bit more often, depending, again, on how the statistics are tabulated and what definitions are used.

So the operative question is not, given a male child molester, how likely it is that he is heterosexual or homosexual, but, given a homosexual man or a heterosexual man, how likely is it that he will molest a child? And we stipulate also that we are not talking about incest, since, again, when you are assessing threats to your children, you can be confident about your own behavior; it's the behavior of other people you must worry about. I will add, though, that as the falsehood called gay marriage grows more commonly accepted, and as people bring into the home children that are not theirs, and that they cannot even adopt as theirs by pretending that they have given birth to them after the exemplary pattern of nature, we will find cases of "incest" spreading like a fungus. It will be more common, far more common, in the unnatural situation than in the natural. There are special reasons for my prediction. Some of them have to do with the sharply increased danger that children are always in when they live with an adult who is not related to them by blood, always excepting heterosexual couples devoted to one another, who cannot have children, but who do the child-making thing, and who thus engage in the saving fiction that the adopted baby may as well have been theirs as anyone's. Some of the reasons have to do, however, with the etiology of unnatural sexual obsession.

But my point here is of general application. Place the condition where it belongs. If we are evaluating the moral behavior of pirates, we do not want to know how likely it is that a ship sunk at sea in the days of the great mercantile navies was sunk by men flying the Jolly Roger. Storms can do the job too. We want to know how likely it is that men flying the Jolly Roger would attack and sink a merchant ship at sea. Of course, for *other reasons* we might want to know about the first likelihood, if what we are considering is not the morality but the relative threat posed by pirates as compared with storms or icebergs or rocks in the shallows of a bay. We must know what we are looking for, and how to find it.

Pay Attention to Opportunities

Let us suppose you are playing poker. You want to know what the odds are, if you draw five cards, that you will get at least three aces. They are not difficult to calculate:

$$4/52 \times 3/51 \times 2/50 \times 10 = 2/1105$$

I will spare the reader the explanation. Now suppose you decide that deuces and threes will be wild. That triples the number of aces in the deck. Does it triple the odds? Let's see:

$$12/52 \times 11/51 \times 10/50 \times 10 = 110/1105$$

Triple? It multiplies the odds by 55.

Now, the aces or the wild cards passing for aces have no knowledge of one another. They do not act by imitation. They do not react by rejection or withdrawal from the game. Human beings do. Imagine that as many as one person in one hundred, on a certain two-lane divided highway, will cross the center line in the path of oncoming traffic. You may suppose that the highway will quickly become notorious for its blood. But you may not suppose that it will stay that way. For people will change their behavior. They will not use the road. Accidents on it will go down, eventually, not up. Yet, it would not be to the road's credit.

"Killer 22," they used to call the U.S. highway in its winding stretch past the cliffs of Bethlehem, Pennsylvania, into and past Allentown. Until there was a better alternative, people had to use the road, and you could tell the accidents from the streaks of car paint left on the center divider and the crushed guard rails to the side. But the alternative, when it was built, siphoned off much of the traffic. It did not mean that 22 was suddenly a better road. It was still awful. But there were fewer opportunities for harm, and any single accident would probably involve fewer cars and fewer casualties.

More boys than girls will end up in the hospital from falling out of a tree, but that does not mean that girls are better than boys at climbing trees. The reverse is the case: boys are a lot better than girls at that, and they are a lot more likely to be in the tree to begin with. Cripples do not fall out of trees at all, because they cannot climb them at all; their complete incapacity means that they will never be in that particular danger. This principle, too, is of broad application. Suppose, because of widespread crime and social chaos, or even because of the perception of it, people stay cooped up in their houses, and children are expected to be overseen by adults during those rare times when they are permitted to play outdoors. The statistical result may well be that crimes against children outside the home will drop to near zero. But what does it mean? That people are kinder to children than they used to be? Not at all. They may in fact be crueler. But they lack the opportunity to put their cruelty into action. You have bought a smallish increase in safety at the expense of freedom, initiative, and a real child-life.

When we assess the meaning of any statistic or any observation of human behavior, we must take into account the available opportunities for it. There may be several reasons why we find no Michelangelo among the Eskimos, but the most obvious ones have to do with opportunity and means. Where is the marble to be quarried, and with what tools?

Where can you get the tools necessary, when you cannot mine the ore under the permafrost? You might as well ask for vintners and traders in olive oil north of the Arctic Circle. More men than women beat people up in brawls, by far, because men *can* do so, and most women cannot, just as more young men than old men can drag you into an alley and rob you, and it is not that old men do not have violent passions, but that they lack the capacity to put them into action. And if they do lack the violent passion, it is not that they are more saintly than young men are, but that their systems have grown cooler; violent crime requires real heat. The sins of old men are less likely to make it to a police report. The same may be said of the sins of women.

Pay Attention to Definitions

Certain falsehoods are like the shell games that swindlers used to set up to trap the unwary. You watch the swindler's hands and you are sure that the pea is underneath this or that shell, when all along he has led you to believe so, while transferring it to another, or in fact letting it drop unseen into his lap. For the liar, or the dupe who spreads bad information, it involves a confusion of terms, so that you intend one thing while the term you use names something else.

Suppose, for example, we are asking ourselves about the number of murders each year in a given nation. What do we want to know? Simply, how many people are deliberately done to death at the hands of others, outside of legal executions. But where can we find that number? Will it include—as we assume it should include—all homicides, and not just those that qualify under the legal definition of murder? Will it include—and I believe it should include—acts of abortion and euthanasia, regardless of their legality? What does the term mean? How are the actions counted?

I have heard it said that American women are now far more educated than they were a hundred years ago, and that that is a good thing. Knowledge and skills are good things, no doubt of that, and women ought to have them. But on what basis do we make the claim? We commonly define education as that which you receive by a certain number of years of schooling, and, more specifically, we define higher education as what you procure at certain venues, such as universities, medical schools, law schools, business schools, and so forth. But notice that the definition has slid. I do not want to know how many people, men or women, go to college. I want to know about their education: about what they know and what they can do. That is a very different thing. I have old books for machinists and electricians — tradesmen who would not have had any college education — that are far too sophisticated for most college students to read. I have heard of students in graduate school complaining that *The Federalist* was too difficult for them to read comfortably, students who were not aware that the essays of Hamilton, Madison, and Jay were first printed as broadsides to be read by a nation of farmers, fishermen, tradesmen, and merchants. Why, opposition to the Federalist position came from, among others, the notorious "Pennsylvania Farmer." We still do not know who he was. Letters and diary entries written by infantrymen in the Civil War impress us with their elegance and sophistication. We should not be surprised; their minds were full of the thoughts and the rhythms of the King James Bible, and what novels they read would have been written by the likes of Henry Fielding and Walter Scott, and those works, too, would be daunting for college students now. What, then, makes us so confident that we are more learned than those soldiers were?

Sometimes the older definition needs to be discarded or altered in order to capture what it used to capture, under new forms and in new circumstances. Take the divorce rate in America. It has leveled off, at somewhere short of 40 percent. That is cold comfort. The rate is ghastly. When the Divorce Reform League was established in 1885, it was because the divorce rate had risen to what was held to be a socially disruptive 10 percent. Be that as it may, can we at least hold that the disruptions of the sexual revolution have settled down, so that we need no longer worry about divorce? Hardly.

For what is it that we want to know, when we are asking about divorce? Not how many legally established marriages break up, but the whole picture regarding the relations of men and women, and their begetting children and caring for them as mothers and fathers together, committed to one another for life. If no one marries, then no one divorces; but we would never call that an improvement over a condition in which everyone marries and a small number of couples divorce. Suppose we consider instead what I have called an Index of Social Dissolution, involving *all male-female relationships of more than five years*, regardless of legal marriage, and *all male-female relationships of more than two years, wherein a child is begotten.* Suppose we ask how many marriages and such quasi-marriages break up. The rate will be frighteningly high, far more than 50 percent, with no likelihood of reduction except by the wholly unacceptable expedient, that men and women should no longer come together in love to begin with.

Then there are definitions that are themselves lies, not because they cover too much or not enough, or because they mistake the reality they are supposed to describe, but because what they purport to define *does not exist*, and even sometimes cannot possibly exist. I must again refer to sexual matters, not because they are the main arena for human falsehood and foolishness but because we, here and now, happen to have gone mad on their account. Take for example the so-called transsexual. Now, it is a matter of plain biological reality that you can no more make a man into a woman, or a woman into a man, than you can make a cat into a dog. The masculinity and femininity of a human person—barring the very rare freak of nature, a birth defect that makes one's sex somewhat ambiguous, or that results in a body that does not possess any functional sex organs at all—is marked upon every cell of the body.

I hope it is not too tedious to get into the details. The boy has an extra layer of skin, making him, literally, thicker-skinned than his sister, and perhaps thus less sensitive to the cuts and scratches he will get in his more aggressive play. His brain organization is not like his sister's, and the differences show up in characteristic ways, for example in his relative slowness of speech, and his relatively deft capacity to rotate three-dimensional objects—a tendency also toward abstraction. The boy baby in the crib will gaze rapt at a mobile above him, with many objects moving simultaneously in a variety of directions; the girl baby is more apt to gaze rapt upon the human face. The male has a larger heart than the female, fit for running and for sudden bursts of muscular force; his aerobic capacity at age forty is still superior to that of the woman at her peak, and will be so for roughly another ten years. He has thicker muscles, and a greater portion of the fast-twitch variety, again fit for those bursts of force. It is why a man in a physical confrontation with a woman can "surprise" her with a blow that seems to come from nowhere, without preparation, without a windup. His bones are thicker, and less prone to fracture: and in fact, boys—barring some factor that gets in their way, such as poor eyesight, a neurological hypersensitivity, or hurtful experience—will gravitate toward rough play just as young bucks like to lock horns, and the play bruises their bones and causes the bones to grow stronger in response. None of this is altered by someone's say-so. Nor is it altered by the amputation of a healthy sex organ, or the attachment of some mockery of a sex organ that is, in its essential function, no more a real organ than a wooden stump is a leg. *There is no such thing as a man who has become a woman, or a woman who has become a man.* There is no "transition."

It will often happen that a definition harbors within itself an unacknowledged and undemonstrated premise: it begs the question. To speak most precisely, I do not oppose a man's marrying another man. I say that it is an impossibility, a contradiction in terms. Sexual intercourse—the congress of the sexes—between them is impossible. They can only do things that mimic intercourse, for the genuine act can only be completed between a living and mature human male and a living and mature human female. To pretend that a man *can* marry another man is to engage in a redefinition that makes no biological sense, locating marriage not in any physical fact but in the mere emotions and the arbitrary imaginations of the actors. It will follow, of course, that everyone will be the readier to dissolve what has for its binding force no more than feelings and fantasies, and that this readiness will influence everyone, including those who are genuinely married.

A definition may also be euphemistic, a lie that deflects attention away from reality and toward a desired sentiment. Ed Norton of happy memory called himself a "sanitation engineer," rather than a fellow who worked in the sewer. It is sometimes said that people name roads after what they destroyed in order to lay them down. I once lived on Bubbling Creek Road, and if there ever had been a bubbling creek nearby, I never found a trace of it. These are humorous cases, but others are not so. In that fine work of contemporary social commentary, *Nineteen Eighty-Four*—for he was not predicting what would happen, so much as noting what had already happened—George Orwell gives us a Ministry of Love that is all about hatred, cruelty, treachery, and torment; a Ministry of Truth, based on his own experiences at the BBC, that is all about obfuscation, lying, and sending uncomfortable evidence of lies and of disapproved events in the past down the "memory hole," a tube ending in an incinerator; and a Ministry of Peace that is all about war, ceaseless war, war mainly to keep the people impoverished and under strict control. America's Department of Education has very little to do with truth, goodness, and beauty, and imparting wisdom to young people, but a great deal to do with compelling the schools of a formerly free people to adopt the approved positions on controversial social matters, or to adopt curricular materials peddled by corporations that take advantage of a captive market.

A doctor who gives you morphine to drug you into a sleep, mixed with poison to kill you, is not acting as a doctor but as a murderer, regardless of your asking him to do so. There is nothing "medical" about his action. It remediates nothing: it restores no function to a sick organ or a broken limb; it drives out no disease; it eases pain only by easing the sufferer out of the world entirely, which is no more than a bullet in the brain might do, with greater disturbance to the chair and the wall and the floor, but with far less disturbance to the social order and the moral laws whereby it subsists. Similarly, abortion is not "medical" but pseudo-medical; the desire is not to heal but to kill.

It has often been said of the Holy Roman Empire that it was neither holy, nor Roman, nor an empire. Many "public servants" in our time are not public—since we seldom know who they are and we have no means of holding them to account for their decisions or actions—or servants but rather concealed rulers, operators of bureaucratic levers behind the scenes. Colleges promote "diversity," which in practice is but forty shades of pink; if they wanted the only form of diversity that an educational institution ought to welcome, namely diversity of thought in pursuit of truth, they would not hound people out of their jobs for daring to cross them in the accepted social fads of the day.

Keep Your Eye on the Ball

Human actions and motives are usually a muddle, and let no one suggest to you otherwise. Mature people learn to distinguish, in their appraisal, persons, motives, judgments, and actions. Let us run through the possibilities.

A good person can support a good thing for good reasons: Mother Teresa petitions the Indian government for a place where she and her sisters can tend to the poor and the dying. A good person can support a good thing for bad reasons: Thaddeus Stevens wants to abolish slavery to punish the southern slaveholders and to extend the power of northern expansionists. A good person can support a bad thing for good reasons: George McGovern wants to expand the reach and power of the state in order to put all men to work. A good person can support a bad thing for bad reasons: Bill Gates, assuming that he is a good man, pushes the Common Core in order to standardize education in America.

A good person can oppose a good thing for good reasons: Patrick Henry fights against the proposed Constitution because he fears that it will demolish the states (which did come about, long afterward). A good person can oppose a bad thing for good reasons: Pope John Paul II inveighs against abortion because it is homicide, and its acceptance cheapens human life. A good person can oppose a bad thing for bad reasons: Daniel Berrigan opposes the Vietnam War more from dislike of America than from love for Vietnam. A good person can oppose a good thing for bad reasons: Jimmy Carter opposes Ronald Reagan's forthright attempt to bankrupt the Soviet Union, because he cannot let go of his personal animosity.

A bad person can support a good thing for good reasons: John Brown calls for abolition because he wants men to be free. A bad person can support a good thing for bad reasons: Hitler builds the Autobahn to facilitate the movement of German troops. A bad person can support a bad thing for good reasons: Lyndon Johnson prosecutes a disastrous war in Vietnam in order to halt the spread of Communism. A bad person can support a bad thing for bad reasons: Stalin engineers a famine in the Ukraine in order to break the kulaks and gather more power to himself and his party.

A bad person can oppose a good thing for good reasons: Woodrow Wilson at Princeton abolishes the fraternities in order to make the school more open to all, regardless of class. A bad person can oppose a good thing for bad reasons: Hugh Hefner does what he can to corrupt men's imaginations, to make a mockery of chastity before marriage and fidelity within it. A bad person can oppose a bad thing for good reasons: Nikita Khrushchev sees the evils of Stalinism and moves to ameliorate them. A bad person can oppose a bad thing for bad reasons: Mitch Snyder opposes homelessness out of hatred for his country, abandoning his own family in his protest.

I do not require the reader to agree with me in these assessments. That is not the point. If you wish, you can come up with your own cases to illustrate the sixteen possibilities. The point is that these possibilities do exist, and that all attempts to deflect attention from person to motive, or from the moral quality of an action considered in itself to the motive of the person supporting it or opposing it, are falsehoods, swindles, regardless of whether the arguer is aware of it. But in our time, these deflections are embedded in the very words we use, and that makes it nearly impossible for us to think rationally about the subject at hand, while sowing the field of debate with land mines.

If John says, "I believe that homosexual action is unnatural and immoral, and its acceptance undermines marriage and the common good," it is a kind of lie for Michael to say that John is a "homophobe." First, John may have no fear of the business at all, and perhaps no disgust, either; nor is it clearly a good thing if he does not feel disgust. Second, it is not to the point. What John says must be evaluated on its merits, as if the saintliest and kindliest man in the world had uttered it; not that saintliness and kindliness make what he says true, either. To use the word *homophobe* is to tell a lie, and to poison the well. If you do not know that your opponent has evil or disreputable motives, but you affirm that he does have them, you are a liar, and at that point no one should credit what you say.

These lies can take on a positive form too. They are lies nonetheless. The Patriot Act had nothing to do with patriots, but the label suggested that those who opposed it were not patriotic. The Affordable Care Act did not actually make health care affordable, but the label probably did serve to dampen opposition. The Respect for Marriage Act enshrined in law a central and deadly attack on marriage, by rendering it a matter of sexual desires and amatory feelings that may come and go, severing it from biological realities and ignoring the rights that children have to a mother and a father both. If we begin to speak the language of such slogans, whether it is laced with acid or sprinkled with sugar, we render ourselves less and less able to think. We spread lies. If we are not aware of our falsehood, let God judge how culpable we are, but the lies do their harm even so.

Falsehoods and "Reason"

When Aeschylus staged the magnificent trilogy we know as the *Oresteia*, Athens had recently undergone a radically democratic reorganization that had as much to do with reorienting men's allegiances as with the mechanics of voting and governance. For men will naturally prefer their own kin and their own interests, and the religious demands that bind them to those who share their blood are strong and not to be dismissed. The usually aristocratic opponents of Athenian democracy looked upon it as a kind of blasphemy. The gambit, as Aeschylus saw it, was this. Athens must put her trust in reason and a spirit of fairness, as embodied in the Athenian assembly that acts as the jury for the case against Orestes, who slew his own mother Clytemnestra for her having slain his father, Agamemnon, after she had taken a lover, Aegisthus, a man who had his own blood feud to prosecute against Agamemnon his cousin, and the house of Agamemnon's father Atreus. Nor did Clytemnestra act without cause against Agamemnon, who had, against his will but pressured by the captains of the army he had mustered, sacrificed their daughter Iphigenia to still the headwinds against them as they prepared to sail to Troy, to take back the adulterous Helen, Clytemnestra's sister and the wife of Agamemnon's brother Menelaus.

The whole story is one of passion and overreach, of cold plotting and raging fury. Orestes must avenge his father; that is the demand of piety. But his own mother is the culprit. What are the claims of blood and family? What does reason say in the case? How do we snap the bonds of vengeance upon vengeance?

Apollo is the defense attorney, smug, slick talking, "reasonable," if by reason you mean that he sometimes does have the right argument, and sometimes not, but you dress up a weak argument in fancy dress, and you hope the jury will not notice. The Furies are the prosecutors, ever ready to fly into a passionate rage, seething under the offense done to their very beings, because they uphold the deep and mysterious claims of blood. Athena is the judge, and when the jury is deadlocked, she casts the tie-breaking vote: to acquit. But when the Furies fly into outbursts of despair, she mollifies them, promising to them too an honored place in the city. For their claims on men's actions must also be acknowledged. So honored, they become the *Eumenides*, the "Kindly Ones." We might say that it is not reasonable in man to be rationalistic.

For the heart has its reasons, that the head knows nothing of, as Pascal says. By *heart* he does not refer to sentiments. He means that we are to see things by the very core of our beings, by an immediate act of the intellect, and not just by rational deduction from premises, or by calculation. And we should keep in mind who is saying this: one of the most brilliant mathematicians who ever lived, the father of probability theory. Pascal understood and saw through the kind of rationalism that Apollo pretends to, as Aeschylus himself did. It is the sort of thing that prevents us from understanding many things that are clear to ordinary people: we "reason" ourselves into falsehoods. And there is another odd thing about it too. Aeschylus's Apollo is by no means a dispassionate fellow, as much as he prides himself on his clear vision. Scratch a rationalist, and you will find many a passion he does not acknowledge. The problem is not that he has passions. He should have them. The problem is that he pretends not to have them, and in so pretending, he does not examine what they are, how potent they are, where they are directed, and whether they themselves are reasonable. Then we get the worst of both reason and passion: the badly reasoning rationalist, devoured by passions to which he is blind. That still does not imply that what he says is wrong. He may be telling the truth in any case. But it does make it hard for him to see the truth. He will fall for lies, and he will be eager to spread them.

I think, in this regard, of the owners of a bakery in Oberlin, Ohio, minding their own business—minding it, that is, keeping watch over it, providing people with good things to eat, but also making sure that shoplifters did not put them out of business. A college boy tries to buy a bottle of wine, using a fake ID, and concealing two more bottles under his jacket. The clerk, a member of the family, rejects the ID and tries to take a picture of the shoplifter. He gets a cuff in the face for his pains. Then he runs after the young thief and tries to hold him until the police come. The thief is joined by two of his friends, female, and they throw the clerk to the ground and start kicking and punching him. That is what was going on when the police arrive on the scene.

Anyone in his right mind should see that the college students are behaving like criminals, and in a mean and cowardly way, to boot. It is one thing to try to pinch wine from a store. That should be enough to get you a suspension from school at least. But to subject the clerk, who was acting reasonably and within his rights, to battery? That, I would think, merits expulsion, and a swift notice from the college administration to students: if you do this, we want no part of you.

As my American readers may well know, the reasonable thing did not happen, because the owners of the bakery, without the slightest evidence, *and without any bearing on the merits of the case at hand*, were accused of racism, and a protest was led against them by a college official. The family brought the college to court, and after several years, much anguish, and the death of the eldest owner, who did not live to see justice done, they won their suit, which cost the college nearly $40 million.

We may boggle at the sheer stupidity — a criminal stupidity, a breach of fiduciary trust between the college and her donors, and an arrogant attack on the mere mortals with the effrontery to dwell in her environs — of the college's actions. But it is not an ordinary stupidity. The ordinarily stupid person is very slow to see things, and there are some things he does not have the wherewithal to see at all. He is to most of us, in many common things, as most of us are to, say, the boy Pascal in his playing with conic sections. This is an *extraordinary stupidity*, one that is not explicable by nature alone. It can come about only by a mechanically predictable ratiocination, trammeled up in a factory whose machines are theoretical lies and half-truths, and fueled by unacknowledged passions, such as envy, hatred, and cruelty. Only a "reasoner" could ever turn that incident of shoplifting into a grand and righteous cause *against the victims*. Only the lies enwound with theory could do it. Nor should we expect that the reasoners will experience any qualms of shame. They break eggs to make omelets, they will say. One of the two principal college agents most to blame in the fiasco has gone on to a brighter and more lucrative job in higher education, at another school.

We should "rain fire and brimstone" on the bakery, said one of the agents. Apparently, a couple of cracked vertebrae were not sufficient punishment for a man who tried to restrain a robber. But the woman's language was telling. People in the grip of rationalized ideological unreason tend to lose all sense of proportion and irony. In the account in Genesis, it is the townsmen of Sodom who beat on Lot's door, demanding, in their sexual aggression, that he release to them the two young men who have come to his house, so that they may "know" them, that is, so that they may rape them (cf. Gen. 19). Lot is not the aggressor. Lot is merely trying to mind his own business. The fire and brimstone the Lord rained down on Sodom was in punishment for their flagrant and unnatural wickedness. What flagrant and unnatural wickedness was the store clerk guilty of? I doubt very much that either the robber, his accessories after the fact, or the dean herself would like to be robbed, or to be beaten if they attempted to resist the robbery and seize the robber. But the dean, without a trace of self-consciousness, adopted for herself the role of God almighty, evidently looking forward with a ferocious glee to the punishment she would engineer.

She exhibited quite the religious and pharisaical zeal. But there is a crucial difference between what she did, fired by the false religion of her ideology, and what a Christian angry at an offender would do if he were hurt unjustly yet he kept his faith in mind. The Christian should know, and had better remember, that all have sinned and fallen short of the glory of God. The Christian should recall the dread words of Christ, who says that if you do not forgive those who sin against you, the Father will not forgive you either, for with what measure you measure, so shall it be measured out to you (cf. Matt. 6:15, 7:2). The Christian is aware that without the grace of God, he might be standing in the dock instead of the malefactor. But none of this is present to the ideologue. He is caught in the toils of a lie, that he is justified merely because he holds the correct ideological beliefs. Therefore it is that ideologues with brotherhood on their lips may harbor murder in their hearts, and their hands are often quick to act accordingly. In this regard, the history of the last century is a stern instructor.

Follow Science, Not Scientists

I do not at all believe that the empirical sciences are our only means to ascertaining truth. But I do believe that we should respect what they have to teach, most of which, though certainly not all, will corroborate or deepen our ordinary perceptions of how things work and act in the world.

The problem is that scientists are human like the rest of us. I do not merely mean that they make mistakes. I mean that they are motivated by passions: ambition, avarice, stubbornness, pride, envy, and fear—fear of being cast out of the inner circle, the people in the know, and being ridiculed for not going along with the prevailing views. They are, like the rest of us, apt to exaggerate what they are certain of, and to exaggerate the probability of what they admit they are not certain of. They are, like the rest of us, apt to find what they have determined to look for from the outset, and not apt to find what they have not determined to look for. They are apt to adopt explanations that do not make them otherwise uncomfortable. In groups, they, too, can behave like mobs. For a mob, unlike a natural organism, is in intelligence always far less than the sum of its parts, and people will behave in mobs as bullies, cowards, ruffians, and cretins, who would in private life be perfectly sensible and gentle. I do not mean to say that what the mob insists on is necessarily untrue. But to the mob, truth no longer matters; getting their way is all in all.

Whenever I see people behaving as mobs, I try to put some intellectual distance between myself and them. If I began by believing as they do, I begin to wonder whether we are correct after all. If I began by doubting what they believe, I begin to wonder whether I should reject it outright. Just as you should not expect cunning, evil intent, and the promotion of falsehood from a group of people engaged in a calm and civil discussion of some important matter (though you may get it anyway), so you should not expect truth from a mob (though they may be in the right). Since you must choose some expedient—since you must live in the world, as you have no divine vantage from which to sift through a mass of often confusing and conflicting information—it is wise to choose against the mob.

I have written many books and articles, not one of which, to my memory, has been about climate change. I am not a meteorologist, and if I were, I would hope to be chaste in my pronouncements, as meteorology is a science still in its infancy. I am not a geologist, an archeologist, an agronomist, or an astrophysicist, whose fields all bear upon the matter and what man might do to address it, if need be. But I am wary of people who say they are certain that the earth is warming considerably, that man is primarily responsible for it, that it is a dire thing, and that we can do something about it that will not make other important and human things even worse. I do not say that a Greta Thunberg, the young Swedish climate-scold, is a liar. Not exactly; but she has no call to rail as she does, and no grounds upon which to declare her certainty. When she does claim certainty, while knowing at heart that she is none of the things I say I am not, she shows that conquest, not truth, is her aim.

Meanwhile, the magic cloak of "science" is donned to justify the most outrageously silly things in the world, while scientists them-selves, as most of them share the secular views of those who don the cloak, are complicit by silence or by encouragement. Whenever you are arguing about the morality of an action, and your opponent plays the Scientific Trump Card, you should understand it as a lie, a fiction. The abuse of certain bodily organs sets male homosexuals up for a range of rare and debilitating and sometimes deadly diseases, but you will never hear "science" invoked against sodomy. Filling your body with synthetic sex hormones, which are growth hormones too, will tend to grow cells you do not want to grow, such as cancer cells, but you will never hear "science" invoked against the Pill. Abortion cuts a woman's pregnancy short while her breast cells are in mid-metamorphosis, and that might also give us pause; but you will never hear the "science of women's health" invoked against abortion. Political passion will trump scientific honesty, and it will even smother scientific inquiry. If you are determined not to see something, you will not see it.

All People Who Shout Are Liars—Almost

I concede: not all people who shout, their faces red with passion, usually of the unpleasant varieties, are liars. You will sometimes have cause to shout from the housetops. But the common connection between shouting and falsehood is worth investigating. And by *shouting* here I include all elements of force, all veiled threats, all insults, and all incessant repetition that will not let you alone. It is not the decibels alone that make up the shout.

Imagine a group of mathematicians trying to discuss how to determine geodesics on a cone—straight lines between two points. The cone was defined and investigated by mathematicians more than two thousand years ago, so you might think that the answer was ready to hand, or easy to calculate if not. But the cone is full of surprises. As it grows steeper, the number of straight lines between two points increases without bound. It's a lovely thing to consider, and it requires calm deliberation and clarity. Now imagine that the same mathematicians, attempting the same work, and without any trace of animosity, are *shouting* at one another. Will the work get done? Won't we suspect that the sheer noise will obstruct clear thinking?

Imagine then that the shouting begins *to produce in the heart the animosity it suggests.* Soon we will have the mathematicians throwing pencil holders at each other, standing on tables, ripping up notebooks, and suggesting that their enemies cannot tell time on an analog clock. It is not propitious for the cause of truth.

When you have no case, say the lawyers, you shout. Liars thrive on noise, because it obstructs or distracts the power of reason. Two cars have collided on the street, and the drivers are shouting at each other, hurling unenviable epithets about the moral behavior of their female progenitors. If you are a policeman, the first thing you need to do is to get them to calm down. Then you might just be able to ferret out the truth. In this case, the person who is last to stop shouting is more likely to be at fault: he has to shout down his own shame.

My point here has to do not with such unfortunate interchanges, but with the whole quality of what we hear and read in the news—and what we read in many textbooks too, and online. We have gotten used to shouting, and since everyone is doing it, we learn to behave as if the gross exaggerations and distortions that shouters engage in are revelations of truth, when actually they make truth nearly impossible to discover. Even the threat of a shout tends to blunt the mind. Many students in our schools sense that if they *do think*, they may speak, and if they *do speak*, they will be shouted down, reviled, even threatened with personal or institutional penalties. So they back down, and that extends all the way to the first tentative beginnings of thought.

Yet many social and political questions require painstaking, slow, humble, tentative analysis, a suggestion here, a reservation there, a doubt about unintended consequences, another doubt about where the premises of a proposed action may lead, a third doubt about balancing costs and benefits; and as long as you have people shouting, as long as you prevent people from doing the dull but necessary work that their positions as guardians of the common good demand, you will get bad law, foolish or mendacious politicians, and more than the usual hatred and enmity searing like flaming swords through the body politic. And in our time, almost everything you will read on an editorial page is a shout: not the result of care, broad experience, deep thought, calm scholarship, but rather of political and sexual passions; the result of lust, ambition, avarice, and all the rest. Nor be fooled by language couched in caustic humor. Many people will lie or will keep from uttering what they see of the truth, borne down by the prospect of becoming the butts of insult and jest. Peter and all the other apostles but John fled from beneath the Cross. We are not told why they fled. Perhaps they fled for their lives, and John, if he was yet a beardless youth, might not have stood in the same mortal danger. But perhaps they fled because they could not bear the mockery. "Insults have broken my heart," pleads the psalmist, "so that I am in despair" (Ps. 69:20). People used to be shamed from telling lies. Now they are shamed from telling the truth. But I suppose that is not a new thing in the world, either. What is new may be the immense power and reach of the threats.

Bad Faith

One final form of the lie is especially dangerous for those who take on trust that the people they engage in argument genuinely want to find the truth. We can call "bad faith" the pretense that you care about the truth of a matter, when either you do not really believe the truth can be found or, more likely, you are going to do or say what you please in any case, so that, for you, the debate is a mere tool to sow doubt in the minds of others, or to distract everyone from your intentions.

It should be obvious that there is no point in arguing with someone who does not care what the results of the discussion may be, except that you may be overheard by others who do care, and you do not want it to appear that you have no reasons or no evidence for what you hold as truth. Many years ago, I tried to engage some protestors at my college in a discussion about what it means to study other cultures, as they had been inveighing against the requirement that they study those dozen or so cultures that have made up what we call Western civilization. I suggested that we read, together, a charming mystical text from the Christian medieval tradition, alongside the ancient Chinese *Tao Te Ching*. For my pains, I was ridiculed in a scurrilous and anonymous letter to the student newspaper. It then became clear to me: the students had been arguing in bad faith. They did not want what they said they wanted. They may not have been conscious of the falsehood. Very often, people who argue in bad faith simply do not examine their own motives. Given the opportunity to suggest texts from other cultures not covered, at that time, in the program they opposed, they came up with nothing, not even after having been invited and even urged to do so. Culture as such, as different as a culture might be from their own, did not interest them. Protesting did.

A current Catholic bishop in the United States wishes to argue that certain sexual practices once regarded as immoral, even repugnant, are to be regarded as morally trivial. He attempts to justify his position by arguments from Church history and from Scripture. But the slovenliness of his arguments gives him away. It is not that he is a stupid man. It is that even if you showed him conclusively that the Scriptures do condemn the behavior, and if you showed him that the Church has been consistent, and uncontroversially so, in its condemnation, he still would not care. He will appeal to certain words of Jesus, taken loosely, as somehow in a vague sense supporting what he wants, without examining them closely, and without bringing them into concord with the whole of Jesus' teachings, let alone the rest of the New Testament.

I can show, from historical and linguistic evidence, and from reading the arguments about the matter at the time, that the Second Amendment to the Constitution of the United States did guarantee to private citizens the right to carry firearms. And many of us are so innocent as to believe that such evidence would matter to judges, politicians, and journalists. To some, yes, but to others, not at all. They will have been arguing in bad faith. Their appeal to the language is strictly a rhetorical and tactical device. Atheists often appeal to Scripture in the same way, either to snipe at believers for supposedly violating the commandments of God or to ridicule what they do not believe in and what they do not trouble to examine closely. If you go on to show them that, no, the early Christians *did not* believe that the six days of creation in Genesis referred to six periods of twenty-four hours, or that, no, Christians are expressly to be held as free from the civic and cultic requirements of the Mosaic Law, as St. Paul specifically says and as is clear from the rest of the New Testament, but that that immunity does *not apply at all* to the moral law, as Jesus Himself always raised the standards of moral behavior in every area of human life, they will laugh at you and change the subject. For they do not really care what Jesus or Paul says. They have been arguing in bad faith.

You may employ arguments from reason and scientific fact to show that the child developing in his mother's womb is a living human being, and that therefore his life should be held as sacred. It may matter to a few people, these arguments; and they must be made, because they deliver the truth. But the fact is, those who support the supposed right to kill the child do not care whether he is a living human being or not. A few are honest enough and cruel enough to say so. Most are not so honest, but your arguing with them will be like shouting against a gale. You may show that the introduction of the birth control pill has been a disaster for the relations between men and women, and for marriage; you assume that your interlocutor cares about both. He does not care. He wants what he wants, and that is that. Some people believe that the temperature of the earth is warming at an alarming rate. By all means, let us have the evidence, and if it is so, and if the warming will be calamitous, and if we can feasibly do something about it without making other matters far worse, then let us act. But there are people who want it to be so, so that they can recommend the thinning out of the human race; and others want it to be so, so they can condemn those they believe to be responsible, whom they hate.

The bad faith does not prove that the arguer's position is incorrect. But it is, as I say, a form of falsehood, a pretense. The fanatic is sometimes right. The skeptic is sometimes merely selfish and obstinate. The person who argues in bad faith may be right, by accident, but his soul is not right, and the worst effect he has on us is not that he wastes our time, but that we may end up imitating him. "Be prepared to make a defense," says St. Peter, to everyone who asks you for a reason for the hope that is in you (1 Pet. 3:15). "Do not throw your pearls before swine," says Jesus (Matt. 7:6). We must heed both commands.

Conclusion

WHAT IS TO be done?

I do not recommend that we make the truth obnoxious, or that we always go out of our way to grapple with people caught up in falsehood. These matters also require prudence and charity. Keep always in mind that someone who believes what is false is in that regard a victim, a sufferer, and that someone who preaches what is false may be doing so with a fairly clear conscience. Yes, there will be villains, persecutors, moral monsters, and outright liars. Most people will not be so.

Yet persons are one thing, and principles are another. Sinners demand our mercy because we are all sinners. But we must be merciless with bad principles, first because we are made for the truth, but second because bad principles do tremendous harm to individual human beings and to the common good. I think we should establish as a law for our behavior that we will neither tell lies nor be a party to lies that others tell. If John changes his name to Daphne, I may, if the circumstances seem to demand it, call him Daphne, if for no other reason than that to call him John might cause confusion. But I will not use the pronoun "she," because that is to be a party to a lie. John is not a woman. He can never become a woman. He can do an imitation of a woman—usually an awkward, foolish, and simplistic imitation. But he is not a woman, and I must not use the pronoun that suggests as much.

I know that I am supposed to believe that one religion is as good as another when it comes to man's approach to God. And in fact I far prefer the company of a devout Hindu from Calcutta than that of a carelessly secular person from Connecticut. In this most important respect, we are kin. I have met Muslims whose devotion to Allah and whose assiduousness in prayer impress me, nor do I wish they were more like the American who passes by a church with a sneer and a shrug. But I am not going to pretend that Hinduism and Islam are not riddled with error. If the devout Muslim were to engage me in conversation about Jesus, I would, I hope, speak frankly and considerately. I will not say, ever, that it is a matter of indifference to God what religion you follow, because that would be to crucify Christ again, to say that His sacrifice was none at all, a mere unfortunate piece of human meanness, and not the ultimate self-giving of God. I would expect, meanwhile, that the Muslim and the Hindu would not treat my own faith with indifference but would respect me enough to wish to correct what they believe to be my errors. Again, they would be closer to me in this than any of us would be to the indifferent, the ignorant, the worldling, and the mocker.

Thought I need not always burden people with what I see, I must never pretend that I do not see it. It would be uncharitable in me at worst, and in bad taste at least, to make a fuss over women in combat during a military parade, or when a woman in uniform is in my company. But I will not be made to say that it is a good thing. I will not deny the sheer physics of it, let alone the anthropology. For man is made to protect woman, not to expose her to lethal harm, and at that without the slightest profit to himself or to his country.

Václav Havel once spoke about the power of a single shopkeeper who one day refused to hang a Communist sign in his window. I want to be like that shopkeeper. To all those who demand that I go along with whatever the economic, political, scholastic, and media powers say is to be believed and uttered by all correct-thinking people, I say no, I must not do that. Christians believe that a forced conversion is no conversion at all. But the worldly powers do not mind a forced conversion. It is often more to their purpose than a confession of genuine belief, because it puts the confessor in a false position: it compels him to feel his own humiliation. It is what Solzhenitsyn said about life in the Soviet Union. The bigger and the more absurd the lie, the more humiliated you are when you utter it, knowing that it is a lie.

What happens to you then? Never think that you can lie with impunity. Every lie you tell, every falsehood you help to cast abroad, every single mean little piece of detraction you enjoy and spread, every cowardly truckling to absurdity, makes you less human, and more like a dumb object, if you retain some embarrassment for being a liar, or like a devil, if you do not. The punishment for the sin is delivered in the sin itself, just as a man who fails to defend a friend he knows is innocent need not wait for retribution; he has already become a coward, and his next act of cringing will come the more easily to him, as will the false excuses, and if it goes on long enough, he will be unable to tell the difference between the true and the false, the courageous and the craven.

Do not be so. Tell the truth, even if sometimes it is by a significant silence and refusal. What if you are the only one? That may happen. But something else may happen too. For man, as I have said, is made by God, who is Truth, and he is made for truth, to rest in it, and to rejoice in it. For peace, as St. Augustine says, is the tranquility of order. You may find others, deeply grateful to you for your courage, and who knows how many of them there will be? The Soviet Union was once thought impregnable. And yet a few short years after Ronald Reagan told the truth about it, calling it an evil empire, much to the consternation of time-serving diplomats and in-the-know journalists, that impregnable fortress fell, and though not one of those diplomats and journalists that I know of went to him to confess that they had been wrong, his words were vindicated.

"If it be so," said the three young men to King Nebuchadnezzar, when he had set up a golden idol for all men to fall down before in worship, and threatened them with death if they would not, "our God whom we serve is able to deliver us from the burning fiery furnace; and he will deliver us out of your hand, O king. But if not, be it known to you, O king, that we will not serve your gods or worship the golden image which you have set up" (Dan. 3:17–18).

For God is light, says the apostle, and in him there is no darkness at all (1 John 1:5).

About the Author

Anthony Esolen is a Princeton graduate, the author or translator of thirty books (including Dante's *Divine Comedy*), and a regular contributor to *Crisis Magazine, Chronicles, Touchstone, Magnificat, American Greatness,* and *Front Porch Republic.* Dr. Esolen is widely praised as one of the best Catholic writers of our age. His engaging, conversational style opens eyes, engages minds, and changes hearts. He has been a professor of English since 1988. He and his wife Debra publish the web magazine *Word and Song,* designed, by means of linguistic history, music, art, classic poetry, and film, to bring to people daily encounters with what is beautiful, good, and true.

Sophia Institute

SOPHIA INSTITUTE IS a nonprofit institution that seeks to nurture the spiritual, moral, and cultural life of souls and to spread the gospel of Christ in conformity with the authentic teachings of the Roman Catholic Church.

Sophia Institute Press fulfills this mission by offering translations, reprints, and new publications that afford readers a rich source of the enduring wisdom of mankind.

Sophia Institute also operates the popular online resource CatholicExchange.com. *Catholic Exchange* provides world news from a Catholic perspective as well as daily devotionals and articles that will help readers to grow in holiness and live a life consistent with the teachings of the Church.

In 2013, Sophia Institute launched Sophia Institute for Teachers to renew and rebuild Catholic culture through service to Catholic education. With the goal of nurturing the spiritual, moral, and cultural life of souls, and an abiding respect for the role and work of teachers, we strive to provide materials and programs that are at once enlightening to the mind and ennobling to the heart; faithful and complete, as well as useful and practical.

Sophia Institute gratefully recognizes the Solidarity Association for preserving and encouraging the growth of our apostolate over the course of many years. Without their generous and timely support, this book would not be in your hands.

www.SophiaInstitute.com
www.CatholicExchange.com
www.SophiaInstituteforTeachers.org

Sophia Institute Press is a registered trademark of Sophia Institute.
Sophia Institute is a tax-exempt institution as defined by the
Internal Revenue Code, Section 501(c)(3). Tax ID 22-2548708.